UNIVERSITY COMMONS DIVIDE

Exploring Debate and Dissent o

In recent years, a number of controversies have emerged from inside Canadian universities. While some of these controversies reflect debates occurring at a broader societal level, others are unique to the culture of universities and the way in which they are governed. In *University Commons Divided*, Peter MacKinnon provides close readings of a range of recent incidents to explore new challenges within universities and the extent to which the idea of the university as a "commons," a site for debate, discussion, and collaboration, may be under threat.

Among the incidents addressed in this book are the Jennifer Berdahl case, in which a UBC professor alleged a violation of her academic freedom when she was contacted by the university's board chair to discuss her blog post speculating on the university president's departure from office; the case of Root Gorelick, a Carleton University biologist and member of the university's board of governors, who refused to sign a code of conduct preventing public discussion of internal board discussions; and the Facebook scandal at Dalhousie University's Faculty of Dentistry, in which male students posted misogynistic comments about their female classmates. These and other examples of turmoil in universities across the country are used to reach new insights on the state of freedom of expression and academic governance in the contemporary university.

Accessibly written and perceptively argued, *University Commons Divided* is a timely and bold examination of the pressures seeking to transform the culture and governance of universities.

(UTP Insights)

PETER MACKINNON is a president emeritus of the University of Saskatchewan and an Officer of the Order of Canada.

UTP insights

UTP Insights is an innovative collection of brief books offering accessible introductions to the ideas that shape our world. Each volume in the series focuses on a contemporary issue, offering a fresh perspective anchored in scholarship. Spanning a broad range of disciplines in the social sciences and humanities, the books in the UTP Insights series contribute to public discourse and debate and provide a valuable resource for instructors and students.

Books in the Series

- Peter MacKinnon, *University Commons Divided: Exploring Debate and Dissent on Campus*
- Raisa B. Deber, *Treating Health Care: How the System Works and How It Could Work Better*
- Jim Freedman, *A Conviction in Question: The First Trial at the International Criminal Court*
- Christina D. Rosan and Hamil Pearsall, *Growing a Sustainable City? The Question of Urban Agriculture*
- John Joe Schlichtman, Jason Patch, and Marc Lamont Hill, *Gentrifier*
- Robert Chernomas and Ian Hudson, *Economics in the Twenty-First Century: A Critical Perspective*
- Stephen M. Saideman, *Adapting in the Dust: Lessons Learned from Canada's War in Afghanistan*
- Michael R. Marrus, *Lessons of the Holocaust*
- Roland Paris and Taylor Owen (eds.), *The World Won't Wait: Why Canada Needs to Rethink Its International Policies*
- Bessma Momani, *Arab Dawn: Arab Youth and the Demographic Dividend They Will Bring*
- William Watson, *The Inequality Trap: Fighting Capitalism Instead of Poverty*
- Phil Ryan, *After the New Atheist Debate*
- Paul Evans, *Engaging China: Myth, Aspiration, and Strategy in Canadian Policy from Trudeau to Harper*

UNIVERSITY COMMONS DIVIDED

Exploring Debate and Dissent on Campus

Peter MacKinnon

UNIVERSITY OF TORONTO PRESS
Toronto Buffalo London

ISBN 978-1-4875-0370-3 (cloth)
ISBN 978-1-4875-2282-7 (paper)

Printed on acid-free, 100% post-consumer recycled paper.

Library and Archives Canada Cataloguing in Publication

MacKinnon, Peter, author
University commons divided : exploring debate and dissent on campus /
Peter MacKinnon.

(UTP insights)
Includes bibliographical references and index.
ISBN 978-1-4875-0370-3 (cloth). – ISBN 978-1-4875-2282-7 (paper)

1. Academic freedom – Canada – Case studies.   2. Freedom of expression –
Canada – Case studies.   3. Freedom of religion – Canada – Case studies.
4. Debates and debating – Canada – Case studies.   5. Dissenters – Canada –
Case studies.   6. Universities and colleges – Canada – Case studies.
I. Title.   II. Series: UTP insights

LC72.5.C3M33 2018   378.1'2130971   C2017-906628-5

University of Toronto Press acknowledges the financial assistance to its
publishing program of the Canada Council for the Arts and the Ontario Arts
Council, an agency of the Government of Ontario.

**Canada Council
for the Arts**

**Conseil des Arts
du Canada**

ONTARIO ARTS COUNCIL
CONSEIL DES ARTS DE L'ONTARIO

an Ontario government agency
un organisme du gouvernement de l'Ontario

Funded by the
Government
of Canada

Financé par le
gouvernement
du Canada

For my granddaughters,
Natalie and Caitlin.
May they find the commons open and inspiring.

Contents

Preface

The commons that is the subject of this book is a platform or space for the debate, discussion, and collaboration that are both inherent in and essential to the idea of the university. This space is multidimensional and has varying degrees of formality. It is to be found in the governance framework and networks; in campus assemblies, associations and clubs; in classrooms, boardrooms, and common rooms; in myriad gatherings of university communities and individuals on and off campus; and in the social media. Its dimensions are physical and hyper-physical, and it is pervasive.

This is the agora of the university, its meeting place, and the centre of its intellectual, cultural, and social life. There are many who meet here. Some of them (students, faculty, staff, administrators, and governors) are frequent visitors; others (invited guests, alumni, supporters, members of the public) are here less often. But all share its space and have interests in its vitality. Some of their shares are specific and relate to particular activities and responsibilities, whether in the classroom, the boardroom, or student meeting; others are general and consist of the interest each participant has in the whole.

This space is essential to life in the academy and to its central mission: seeking truth through advancing knowledge, learning, and discovery. Because it is essential, it must be robust, and safety within the commons must be assured, though comfort within it cannot be. The commons envelops contentious matters, and its occupants are human beings with their many differences.

Contestation is inevitable, indeed definitional, and with it comes unease, discomfort, and dissent.

The nature of a contest matters, however, and must be contextualized. The cases and other examples considered in this book were selected because they fairly portray the divided commons in our academic lives, and because they are known on a conversational level to most Canadians with an interest in our universities. My goals are to move from conversation to analysis, and to contribute to what I hope will be a debate on their meaning. Are they simply passing controversies of little significance to anyone other than the protagonists? To what extent do they reveal a struggle for values, supremacy, or exclusiveness that may diminish our commons, or sidetrack some of its actors? To what extent do they represent change in our universities or higher visibility of their activities now than in the past? Do they illustrate people at work in the agora or actors contributing to its fracture? My central argument is that the case studies and examples inform us that our commons is under threat and that it requires our attention to ensure that it is not weakened.

I acknowledge many contributions to this book, including several from the University of Saskatchewan. Peggy Schmeiser suggested that I explore this subject and provided insights into my proposal and some of my drafts. Michael Atkinson discussed ideas and excerpts with me throughout and, as he has done so often in the past, provided excellent advice and nudged me in the direction of new angles on topics to explore. Lea Pennock brought her fine judgment to a review of my proposal and to two draft chapters, and her ground-breaking work on university senates was influential in my thinking about governance. Karen Chad's irrepressible enthusiasm and provocative questions encouraged me at key stages of the project. University president Peter Stoicheff and his partner, Kathryn Warden, gave me an opportunity to test my thinking with a probing audience at their residence on the university campus. Susan Bertolo, my able assistant for my thirteen years as president of the U of S, prepared the manuscript for submission to the Press.

They were joined by others. Richard Florizone and Mona Holm-lund were early and helpful listeners to my ideas and encouraged me to undertake the project. Tamara Buckwold, Martha Piper, and Michael Wernick provided advice and information at critical junctures. Paul Davidson, Philip Landon, Dwight Newman, and Andrew Prior critiqued draft chapter 5. Agnes Herzberg assisted by proofreading the manuscript. Gail Brennan and Karen Crombie supplied background information and documents. I am indebted to all and I thank them warmly.

My son William brought his discerning eye to a reading of the manuscript. My wife Janice debated many of the issues with me. My brother Philip discussed the commons, or his preferred metaphor – the agora – with me. My granddaughters, to whom this book is affectionately dedicated, and their parents Alan and Anoma, provided welcome respite from my work. To them and to the rest of my family, I will forever be grateful.

I was fortunate once again to be working with the University of Toronto Press. I am particularly grateful to Daniel Quinlan, who responded with enthusiasm to my proposal, read each of the draft chapters, and provided me with excellent and timely advice. Wayne Herrington guided the production process and kept me well informed along the way. Ian MacKenzie's copy-edit was outstanding. The Press's anonymous reviewers, and the reader for the Manuscript Review Committee, offered excellent insights and advice that improved the book. I warmly thank them all, and I alone am responsible for any shortcomings that remain.

UNIVERSITY COMMONS DIVIDED

Exploring Debate and Dissent on Campus

Introduction

Once commonly conceived as ivory towers removed from the forces and pressures of social change, our universities are now in the midst of those influences and sometimes their harbinger. The changes begin with their central actors: professors and students. Faculty members feel they are losing authority over their universities. They place disproportionate responsibility for this loss on the more managerial culture of administrations, though there are greater forces at work that are diminishing their influence. Their universities are larger, more bureaucratic, more impersonal, and less collegial. Governments are more interventionist; their and the public's appeals for transparency and accountability are directed to professors as they are to everyone else. Universities are now heavily regulated and have large cadres of professional and other employees to attend to regulatory matters. Professors have become a minority among their universities' personnel and are surrounded by large numbers of professional and support staff. Most of them have joined unions and, as a result, are treated more as employees and less as self-governing or semi-regulated professionals. And technology has changed their workplaces and relationships with others.

Their students have changed too. There are more of them and they are more diverse. They have been courted by the universities they attend, not simply admitted to them. They are consumers, and their education is a consumable for which they are attentive to price and satisfaction. They seek engagement, active learning, and a collaborative learning environment, not professor-centred instruction. And their interactions – among themselves and with others – are mediated by technology.

The administrators to whom faculty, students, and the public look to lead their universities are in the middle of these changes. Faculty, staff, and students are not their only communities. These can be subdivided within universities into groups that may overlap but have ideological and other differences, and these are only the communities within. Governments, alumni, community members, friends, and supporters bring their interests and perspectives into the mix, thereby increasing the number of voices heard and adding to the complexity of difference.

The framework in which contestation must be accommodated, and balance sought, is the unique governance architecture of universities. Its main feature is a diffusion of authority greater than is found in other large organizations, and its capacity to entertain and adjudicate differences in the commons is under stress. With multiple communities pursuing particular interests, boards and senates now face competition from those who challenge their authority, or seek to share or displace their primacy in governance. The bicameral governance model that has prevailed since the 1966 Duff-Berdahl Report may no longer accommodate the complexity of twenty-first-century universities. And there has been little consideration of alternatives. This development will be a recurring theme as we venture into the agora in the cases and examples that follow.

I should disclose the background that influences the perspectives readers will encounter in this book. In my four decades of university life, I have been a law professor and licensed member of the Bars in Saskatchewan and Ontario, an assistant dean and dean of law, a faculty association chair, an interim vice-president (academic), and, for fifteen years, a university president. I have been chair, respectively, of the Association of Universities and Colleges of Canada (now Universities Canada), the Council of Canadian Law Deans, and the Canadian Association of Law Teachers. From 2012 to 2014 I was the inaugural Prime Ministers of Canada Fellow at the Public Policy Forum, where I wrote *University Leadership and Public Policy in the Twenty-First Century: A President's Perspective*

(University of Toronto Press, 2014). This book examined major issues of public policy that form part of the context in which Canadian universities must do their work and is an important precursor to the present volume.

I approach my task by grounding the discussion and analysis in cases and examples. They are drawn from several universities of different kinds, and from one end of the country to the other. Many are known to Canadians because of the media attention they have received. I begin with the Berdahl case at UBC, in part because it provides continuity with some of my earlier work in the volume mentioned above, and also because some of the analysis is foundational to later discussion on academic freedom and governance. From the Pacific to the Atlantic, chapter 2 takes us into the details and difficulties of the scandal in Dalhousie's Faculty of Dentistry that rocked the university, and attracted national and international attention, in 2014–15. Its broader significance lies in lessons learned about crisis management and in implications for events that invoke questions of discipline.

Chapter 3 is organized around examples from several universities in which freedom of expression is the central issue. Freedom of expression in Canada is enshrined in the Canadian Charter of Rights and Freedoms and, despite questions about the Charter's application to universities, this freedom is either a constitutional right of all in our commons, or a constitutional value commanding high fealty. Moreover, it is central to the mission, obligation, and duty of universities and should be the first principle in their activities. I believe the examples suggest that, in practice, its status is being reduced to one among many considerations in play in our commons. That is not good enough in institutions committed to the search for truth.

In chapter 4 we return to a focus on one case, but its implications are many. Carleton's blogging board member raises issues both of academic freedom and university governance, and allows us to build on earlier chapters that raise these issues. The dispute has attracted the usual interests but their formulaic answers to the questions presented by the case are unsatisfactory. We shall further explore the unique nature of university boards, and the difference between being a faculty member and being a faculty member on a board of governors.

Chapter 5 asks the question whether it is appropriate to include a law faculty among the programs of a private, evangelical university that requires its students to pledge restraint from sexual intimacy outside of marriage between one man and one woman. The case of Trinity Western University raises boundary issues between the public and the private, and between freedom of religion and anti-discrimination laws, and they are not unique to TWU. There are other faith-based institutions in Canada, and the national organization of Canadian universities, Universities Canada, has grappled for years with questions relating to their membership. This chapter will explore these boundary and membership issues, and the broader intersection between the private domain and anti-discrimination laws and policies.

Chapter 6 brings us to broad efforts to welcome Indigenous peoples into the commons, and other movements to exclude industries that produce carbon and genetically modified organisms from it. The chapter invites us to reflect upon a more pervasive regulatory environment that has changed campus life, and altered the composition of the commons. We consider the social responsibility of universities and ask whether it has changed to embrace movements carried on in the name of social justice.

In chapter 7 we return to the agenda for this book and reflect upon the conclusions and directions to which the discussion leads. We shall reflect, too, upon the governance of universities and whether bicameralism as envisaged in the Duff-Berdahl Report is up to the challenge of the politics of difference in our divided commons.

chapter one

Governance and Academic Freedom at UBC: The Jennifer Berdahl Case

In August 2015 the University of British Columbia's thirteenth president became the latest casualty of the precarious presidency.[1] Arvind Gupta resigned after one year in office, triggering speculation about the reasons for and circumstances of his early departure. Among those speculating was Jennifer Berdahl, the Montalbano Professor of Leadership Studies: Gender and Diversity at the university's Sauder School of Business. She opined on social media that the president lost his job because he "lost the masculinity contest," he "wasn't tall or physically imposing," and was the "first brown man to be the university's president."[2]

University board chair John Montalbano – and the donor whose support created the professorship held by Professor Berdahl – phoned the professor to discuss the blog. Another phone call from an unidentified person in the Sauder School's dean's office expressed concern about the school's reputation and fundraising prospects.

The university's faculty association alleged that Montalbano and the caller from the business school dean's office interfered with the academic freedom of Berdahl and breached university policies on respectful environment, employment equity, discrimination and harassment, fundraising and acceptance of donations, and conflict of interest and commitment. UBC and its faculty association retained Lynn Smith, a former BC Supreme Court judge and UBC law dean, to investigate whether the board chair or the business school had violated the collective agreement, any university policy, or the academic freedom of Berdahl.

This case, Smith's findings, and the aftermath raise many questions about board governance, privacy, and the nature of academic freedom. With respect to the first of these, university boards of governors[3] are both similar and dissimilar to boards of other public and private entities. They are led by a chair, usually elected by the board, though sometimes appointed by government. They are accorded latitude in how they conduct their business, and enact bylaws or other rules that guide them in doing so. They follow many of the protocols and practices of board governance generally. But, and here is one big difference from other boards, they have plenary authority only over the university's business affairs. They share governance with those responsible for the university's academic affairs, usually convened as a senate, or in academic councils within faculties.

There is another feature of university boards that we shall encounter in many settings in this book. In addition to the president and representation from internal university constituencies (at UBC two students, three faculty members, and two staff members), there are public members of the board (the chancellor and ten others) who donate thousands of hours over their terms to the university. They are volunteers and are unpaid for their service. In the case of professionals who bill for their time, they – and their professional colleagues – forgo income in the cause of service to the university.

These features of university boards underline a second big difference between them and other boards. Corporate boards know who their shareholders are; so too do boards for not-for-profit organizations. Difficult questions are resolved by reference to shareholder or stakeholder interests, and while these may not always be easily identified, no one doubts their paramountcy in guiding corporate affairs. University boards are not as simple. Shareholders and stakeholders are not as readily determined and indeed may be seen to differ for different board members. All may claim fiduciary responsibility for the best interests of the university, but some are present in representative capacities for students, faculty, sometimes unions or other associations, and the general public.

Who are the shareholders and stakeholders for a board constituted in the name of different constituencies, and how are their interests expressed in deliberations of the whole?

Boards hire presidents or rather have the last say in doing so. A search committee consisting of board members and others within and outside the university consults widely to develop and publicize a position profile identifying the qualities sought in a successful candidate. It then goes in camera to recruit, screen, and interview candidates before bringing one or more names to the board. The board subsequently announces its appointment of a new president with much fanfare and celebration of her suitability for the office.

With dismissals or departures that may have been pressured or encouraged, boards generally act alone and communicate little more than a parting of the ways. When pressed for reasons, they typically cite privacy considerations and declare their unwillingness to discuss personnel matters in public. In August 2015 at UBC, Board Chair Montalbano announced the departure of Gupta as a resignation, a personal and regrettable decision,[4] but within days it was clear that the explanation would not stand unchallenged. Montalbano was quickly under fire for secrecy and his exchange with Jennifer Berdahl, and calls for his resignation came from the faculty association and others.[5] In reply, Montalbano stated that confidentiality arrangements "were entered into and both parties were bound by that arrangement."[6]

The early and abrupt departure of a president naturally generates speculation and controversy within any university. For a university of the stature of UBC, the event attracts wide concern among its supporters and an anxiety among the public about its meaning for the university, and beyond. "What happened?" is a common and pressing question, and questioners are not satisfied by citations of privacy and normal human resources policies. Many of them were engaged in consultations leading to the development of the position profile; they do not want to be left in the dark when one so widely celebrated as an excellent fit only a year earlier suddenly resigns.

But privacy issues are not to be waved aside. Despite the confidentiality agreements between Gupta and the UBC board, UBC's faculty association[7] and some press commentary[8] appealed for transparency and disclosure about the Gupta departure. However, they were advocates for privacy[9] when UBC professor Steven Galloway was suspended months later and fired in the summer of 2016. Galloway was chair of the university's creative writing program when his suspension was announced, pending the investigation of what were said to be serious allegations against him. Retired judge Mary Ellen Boyd was asked to investigate these allegations and others that surfaced following the suspension. Subsequent to her confidential report, UBC's board accepted the president's recommendation for dismissal based on Galloway's "irreparable breach of the trust reposed in him by the university, its students and the public,"[10] and Galloway's appointment was concluded.

Unease about the dismissal has not ended. In September 2016 Hollywood producer Hart Hanson, a graduate of the UBC creative writing program, announced cancellation of a possible contribution to the university and declined its invitation to work with students in the program. He cited concern about the secrecy surrounding the case and his concern that Galloway may not have been fairly treated by the university.[11] Weeks later, writer Joseph Boyden published a letter, supported by many in the Canadian literary community, calling for an investigation into the handling of the case by UBC.[12] This engendered a division of the community into camps of established and emerging writers, and exchanges between them highlighting different perspectives on the Galloway case.[13] The collegiality of the accomplished and tightly knit literary community "has now ruptured. Some long, meaningful friendships have dissolved. The program Galloway once led has ugly scars and deep divisions."[14] UBC remained silent about the case, citing legal obligations and privacy concerns, but Galloway did not. He released a statement confirming a two-year-long affair with a student and stating that he "profoundly regrets his conduct and wishes to apologize for the harm that it has caused."[15] The issues of process and result are expected to be addressed in a grievance arbitration in 2017.[16]

What are the differences between these two cases? What do they tell us about university governance and processes? What guidance do they offer on how similar cases should be addressed in the future?

We begin with the different offices of the two. One was the president, the other a tenured faculty member and program chair. Both were well known, Gupta by virtue of his office, Galloway because he is a prolific and award-winning author. Galloway was dismissed and Gupta resigned, no doubt under pressure from the board. These considerations do not lead to the conclusion that the board and administration should publicly disclose the reasons for their departures or for treating the two cases differently.

Turning to the reasons for departure, our information is incomplete because no official statement disclosing reasons was made in either case. There was speculation, of course, and reports based on unnamed sources began to emerge. However, it can be inferred from what is publicly known that Gupta's departure originated from within the board, while Galloway's emanated from complaints to the administration from third parties. This difference would not justify the board treating the two cases differently by publicly disclosing the reasons for one and not for the other.

The material differences between the two cases are that Galloway was suspended before his dismissal, and the interim president publicly announced his suspension; and Gupta had agreed to a confidentiality pact with the board. These differences lead to the two most important questions in this analysis: Should there have been a public announcement of Galloway's suspension? And does the confidentiality agreement trump other considerations in determining whether the board should have disclosed the reasons for Gupta's departure?

The University of British Columbia Act provides that the president "has power to suspend any member of the teaching and administrative staffs and any officer or employee of the university."[17] The collective agreement between the university and its faculty association defines suspension and sets out the process that is to be followed, and the parties to whom notice of suspension must be given.[18] Neither the Act nor the collective agreement addresses the issue of public announcement of a suspension, and so we must consider possible reasons for it.

We can think of four reasons. First, a suspension might be announced to assure complainants and others affected by the investigation that action is being taken to address the reported behaviours. This is not a compelling reason, because those affected could be informed individually and privately. The second and third reasons are more persuasive. A suspension might be publicly announced to encourage others who may be able to assist in the investigation to come forward. And it might be announced for preventive reasons, as a caution to others who might be affected by a repetition of the reported behaviours.

The fourth and most compelling reason arises from Galloway's position as a program chair with ongoing administrative responsibilities for an academic program. University administrators had to say something to program faculty, staff, and students. Do they say nothing, in line with faculty association thinking? Do they simply announce a suspension without any explanation, or with a proviso that they are unable to disclose anything more than the fact of the suspension? Whatever they say – or don't say – news of the suspension is going to become public, accompanied by speculation about reasons. Whatever the speculation, it would have been obvious that there were underlying reasons or allegations serious enough to call for suspension and investigation.

Are these considerations outweighed by the faculty association's argument that the administration had an obligation to protect Galloway's privacy by refraining from a public announcement of the suspension? We do not have all the information at hand to give a definitive answer, but it would seem that the provisional answer is no. If the interim president had reason to conclude that the suspension should be made public for preventive reasons, to assist in the investigation, or to provide at least minimal information to those immediately affected by the suspension, she was justified in doing so.

We turn now to the other difference between the two cases: the confidentiality agreement between Gupta and the board. Confidentiality may be required of employees in the normal course of their employment, but in this context the agreement requires both parties to remain silent as a condition of a mutually acceptable parting of their ways. The pact may be essential to an end to the employment relationship by agreement rather than one that is disputatious or litigious. Interests of both parties are in play. Perhaps a sum of money will be paid, which an employer does not want to be viewed as a precedent; perhaps the circumstances of a departure involve third parties whose identities should be protected. It may be that employer and employee wish to avoid mutual recriminations in public and after the fact. Or they seek to avoid disclosure because the circumstances of their parting are personal or delicate. It may be, too, that an employee feels that if a parting is inevitable, future employment prospects are better with a quiet resignation rather than a dismissal.

Board Chair Montalbano was quickly attacked for honouring the confidentiality agreement. UBC's faculty association president urged his departure from the office, saying, "We believe it is ... imperative to have the full story behind the resignation of Prof. Gupta as president of UBC."[19] This is tantamount to saying either that Montalbano should renege on the board's commitment or that there should have been no confidentiality agreement at all. The former is unworthy of comment but the latter is not.

What is the "full story" that the faculty association sought to have disclosed? And whose story is it? Montalbano's? The nineteen members of the UBC Board (who may agree with the result but who may not concur in the reasons)? Is it Gupta's story, or that of people who had concerns about his leadership? Is it the story of unnamed sources who have (or claim to have) insider knowledge, or those who construct an account from what is publicly known or assumed? The answer is that there is no single, full story other than the agreed upon departure and confidentiality pact. A failure to reach that agreement would make it more likely that a parting would have been for cause, not a result in anyone's – or in the university's – best interests.

There is another dimension of the confidentiality issue. British Columbia has privacy legislation[20] that provides: "It is a tort, actionable without proof of damage, for a person, willfully and without a claim of right, to violate the privacy of another."[21]

The legislation further provides that the nature and degree of privacy to which a person is entitled is that which is reasonable in the circumstances.[22] In the circumstances of Gupta's resignation, ignoring the confidentiality agreement would have incurred almost certain liability. Without the confidentiality agreement, liability for disclosing the reasons for Gupta's resignation would have been possible, if not probable. The failure or unwillingness of the board's critics – at the university and in the media – to acknowledge or address this legal constraint defies explanation.

Jennifer Berdahl thought she knew the story about Gupta's departure, and she offered the account described at the beginning of this chapter, which ultimately led to the resignation of Montalbano and to the retention of retired judge and former UBC law dean Lynn Smith. Her specific charge was to conduct an independent investigation into whether Montalbano or certain individuals in the school of business "conducted themselves in the events following Jennifer Berdahl's publication of her blog on August 8, 2015 in a manner that violated any provision of the Collective Agreement, the UBC Statement on Respectful Environment, or any applicable university policies including whether her academic freedom is or was interfered with in any way."[23]

Of particular interest are Smith's three conclusions:[24]

(1) UBC failed in its obligation to protect and support Dr Berdahl's academic freedom. The Collective Agreement creates a positive obligation to support and protect academic freedom. Through the combined acts and omissions of Mr Montalbano, the named individuals in the Sauder School, and others, UBC failed to meet that obligation with respect to Dr Berdahl's academic freedom.

(2) Mr Montalbano, on his own, did not infringe any provision of the Collective Agreement, the UBC Statement on Respectful Environment, or any of the applicable university policies.

(3) No individual in the Sauder School of Business, identified by the faculty association, on his or her own, infringed any provision of the Collective Agreement, the UBC Statement on Respectful Environment, or any of the applicable university policies.

When considered in the context of Berdahl's accusations, Smith's findings raise more questions than they put to rest. It could not have been expected – by Berdahl or by anyone else – that her accusations would attract no reply or be lightly brushed off. She accused Montalbano and the board of three damning isms of modern discourse: racism, sexism, and lookism. And while Smith noted that in doing so Berdahl was drawing upon her research, it could not be said she was applying her research to the facts, because she did not know the facts, or at least did not reveal that she knew the facts.

In these circumstances, Montalbano, and others, had three choices: to do or say nothing (which is unrealistic and potentially damaging in light of the severity of Berdahl's charges), to make a public statement refuting them (which would have drawn them and others into a public debate about what did or did not lie behind Gupta's departure), or to express their concerns directly and only to Berdahl herself. If, as Smith found, they did not violate her academic freedom, that should have ended the matter.

But it did not. Smith did not think Berdahl should have been phoned, even though those calls did not violate her academic freedom. What, then, did she expect UBC to do to support and protect Berdahl's academic freedom to publicly accuse Montalbano and others of racism, sexism, and lookism? Should the university have made a public statement to the effect that while the board did not agree with her, it supported and protected her academic freedom to make the charges? Should members of the board and administration have contacted Berdahl to give her positive reassurances or comfort when she made the charges, or subsequently, when or after the callers expressed their concerns? Is an explicit commitment of support and protection for academic freedom necessary whenever a university or board officer expresses disagreement with or concern about a faculty member's public allegations or utterances?

It is true that UBC has a positive obligation to support and protect academic freedom, an obligation it shares with other universities. It means that university officers must honour and value the freedom and publicly confirm its importance through its vigorous defence when it is threatened. No suggestion was made that UBC officials have fallen short in this regard, and it is a stretch to conclude that the obligation is invoked in circumstances where it has been found that no violation of academic freedom occurred.

The differences at UBC illustrate a schism in our commons: there is disagreement about the meaning of academic freedom and the scope of its protection. The two main sides to the disagreement are illustrated by statements on the subject by Universities Canada (UC) and the Canadian Association of University Teachers (CAUT). The former is a membership organization whose members are the ninety-seven public and not-for-profit private universities in Canada, represented in UC business by their presidents. The latter is also a membership organization, whose principal members are the unionized and non-unionized faculty associations across the country. UC sees academic freedom as rooted in teaching and research and the professional scholarly activities necessary to carry them out.[25] CAUT sees it in broader terms that include teaching and research, but extends beyond them to other activities, including criticism of the university and its governance.[26]

Collective agreements specific to particular universities also address the subject,[27] though not usually in terms that exclude other authorities on its scope and extent. And so a debate on the parameters of academic freedom may invoke reference both to particular collective agreements and to the history and evolution of the concept, including decisions over the years on its application and coverage. More will be said on this subject in subsequent chapters, but for now it is sufficient to point out that differences of opinion on the scope of academic freedom can be illustrated with reference to the Berdahl case.

The first argument is that this is not an academic freedom case. In accusing the board chair and board of racism, sexism, and lookism, Berdahl was not engaged in either teaching or research; like others, she was speculating about the reasons for Gupta's departure. In any event, Smith found no infringement of her academic freedom.

An argument that this is not an academic freedom case does not challenge Berdahl's right to say what she said. Freedom of speech is to be cherished in all democratic settings, nowhere more than in universities. There is no doubt about Berdahl's right to speak out about what she understood to be the reasons for Gupta's departure. But there is a difference between academic freedom and free speech. The former bestows protection on the speaker and invokes obligations upon others that are not common to the latter.

The counter-argument is rooted in Berdahl's academic specialty as well as in the broader sweep of the CAUT statement and the UBC Collective Agreement. Berdahl held a chair in leadership, gender, and diversity and so was speculating not as any member of the public, but as one who knows much about these subjects. Further she was speculating about a decision of the board and so was commenting on governance. Under the CAUT statement, criticism of the university and its governance is protected by academic freedom, and Smith read similar protection into the UBC collective agreement.[28]

This counter-argument brings us back to the issue of what is owed to Berdahl in these circumstances. Her academic freedom must not be violated, and it was not. If infringement had occurred or was threatened, it must be defended by the university. She is not owed concurrence, comfort, or gentle rebuttal. She made damning and public allegations against Montalbano and the board. They were entitled to respond and, along the spectrum of possible responses, theirs was restrained: no public indignation or rebuttal; no public criticism of Berdahl for her denunciation of Montalbano and the board when she could not have known all the facts; only phone calls from the board chair (whom she knew) to discuss the blog, and someone in her dean's office expressing their concerns. And again, it must be emphasized, these were phone calls that were found not to have violated her academic freedom. But the episode drove Montalbano from the commons. UBC accepted the findings in the Smith report – there was little choice not to do so – and Montalbano immediately resigned. Simultaneously the university announced a number of measures to better define and strengthen the university's positive obligation to defend academic freedom.[29] The faculty association made the most it could of Smith's report and decided to pursue the board further. Acting on a petition signed by about 15 per cent of the association's more than three thousand members, it sought a declaration of non-confidence in the board of governors, which it ultimately secured on a vote of about 25 per cent of its members.[30] Meanwhile a new search committee was struck to identify Gupta's successor, and Gupta himself stated that he regretted resigning rather than pushing back on the pressure to do so. Jennifer Berdahl was elected as a faculty representative in the search and subsequently resigned, citing non-confidence in the new committee. The faculty association felt the same way and sought a declaration of non-confidence in the committee and the ouster of two of its members, including the university's chancellor. It secured the non-confidence vote upon polling one-quarter of its members. The chancellor and his colleague on the board resisted the pressure to step aside, though the latter ultimately left the board.[31] The new president was announced in the spring of 2016.[32]

We are left with an image of a fractured commons. There are several messages implicit within the narrative, the first of which is that boards confronted by faculty associations struggle with one or both hands tied behind their backs. The UBC board was attacked by Berdahl and by the faculty association, and could not publicly defend itself on the merits because of confidentiality and other considerations. For this reason, as well as the reach of the faculty association within the university, the non-confidence votes were bound to pass. A review of the public record on the Berdahl case and its aftermath reveals the extent to which it was dominated by unanswered attacks on the board and individual board members.

A second message, this one to boards themselves, is that they must reflect upon their disadvantage in any controversy following decisions where their members are bound by confidentiality requirements. They will be vulnerable to questions, criticism, and denunciation that must go unanswered in public, and they cannot rely on informed media coverage to provide perspective on difficult issues. The media are interested in controversy and in who is blaming whom for what, not in governance, the institutional context, or reasons why university and board officials cannot put all they know on the table. This may lead boards to rethink confidentiality requirements on some matters, and here the law of unintended consequences may come into play. Where they conclude that it is in the university's interest for a president to leave office, they might be more inclined in future to dismiss for cause rather than to reach an agreement to part ways under the terms of a confidentiality agreement. This is not a desirable outcome, but it may be a more likely one in view of the Montalbano precedent.

A third message points to the numbers of UBC faculty who were absent from the commons when important decisions were taken by a fraction of their members. The problem is not unique to UBC. Faculty associations have their leaders, activists, and sympathizers, and beyond them are their hundreds of members, thousands even, who pay them scant attention or absent themselves from their deliberations and decisions. But it is in their names too that faculty associations act, and there is a high price paid for their absence from discussion in the commons about the wisdom and fairness of proposed actions.

A fourth message is that academic freedom needs to be more fully understood and framed in ways that prevent a repetition of the UBC case. In this book the ancient agora has been used as a metaphor for our university space or commons. This is our meeting place for the ideas, discussions, and debates in the academy. Academic freedom accompanies some who enter the agora and protects them from infringements upon their scholarship; it does not protect them from reply, contradiction, or criticism. If the import of the Smith decision is that the protection of Berdahl's academic freedom required Montalbano to be silent or deferential in the face of the charges brought against him and the rest of the board, then the decision is unsound. The charges were damning, and he should have had the latitude to answer them – even to Berdahl herself – provided that he did not infringe upon her academic freedom, which he was found by Smith not to have done.

Administrations at UBC and at other universities can at least derive relief from the fact that Smith's decision should not be looked upon as a precedent, except with respect to matters she was asked to decide. She was charged to determine whether there had been violations of academic freedom or university rules or policies, and her answer was no. Her opinion that Montalbano and others failed to protect and support Berdahl's academic freedom is just that: an opinion, or what is known in legal reasoning as dicta – musings on matters not material to answering the question before her. Her thoughts here may be of interest but they are of no standing as precedent.

The last message to be taken from this story is about board governance. At root, this was an attack on the UBC Board of Governors. It began with the faculty association's claim that the board should have disclosed the reasons for Gupta's departure (though the association did not make the same appeal in the case of Professor Galloway only months later). Together with Berdahl's charge that the board was motivated by racism, sexism, and lookism, the attack drove Montalbano from the commons when Smith opined that he failed to support and protect her academic freedom. The attack continued, with no-confidence motions in both the board and the new search committee, and with attempts to sideline the chancellor and another member – attempts that were unsuccessful in the case of the chancellor and successful in the case of his colleague.[33]

This was hardly a context for debate in the commons. Trust matters here – not blind confidence that the right things are being done for the right reasons – but trust in good faith until the contrary is shown which it was not in this case. Proportionality and tone matter too, and both were wanting in the attacks on the UBC board. Its attackers, and the rest of us, should be reminded that university boards have important work to do on behalf of our universities and are vital in the protection of university autonomy. They deserve the same collegial understanding and respect in the commons that are claimed by their critics.

chapter two

Sexual Transgressions at Dalhousie: Dentistry Students on Facebook

Dalhousie University's Faculty of Dentistry class of 2015 included a Facebook group under the name Class of DDS 2015 Gentlemen. The male-only group, with membership by invitation, had been in existence since their first year, and many of their posts were "sexist, misogynistic, and homophobic."[1] The group was exposed when, in 2014, one of its members invited the others to reveal who they would like to "hate fuck" and "sport fuck." Another member – identified in a subsequent report as the whistle-blower[2] – showed the post to a female classmate who was named in the poll and allowed her to take a screenshot of this and earlier posts.

Complaints, reviews, and enquiries ensued as a mounting scandal attracted national and international attention. Police considered possible violations of the Criminal Code,[3] and members of the profession speculated on whether those implicated would be admitted to the profession of dentistry.[4] But when police ruled out criminal prosecution, and the profession deferred because the issue was not yet admission to its ranks, the initiative for addressing and resolving the issues was left in the university's hands.

When the police and profession's gatekeepers bowed out of the controversy, they left other interested parties behind. First, there were female dental students, some of whom were subjects of the Facebook posts, and the group members themselves, all senior students nearing the end of university educations that represented their professional ambitions and an inestimable investment of time and money. Second, there were the members of the broader university community who had an interest in Dalhousie's response to the behaviours; and third, those responsible for taking the lead in that response, primarily the university and dental faculty administrations. Behind them all was the general public, some of whom joined the public and social media dialogue around the scandal, with others watching to see what happened.

We begin with those at the heart of the case: the Facebook group members and those named in their posts. On 8 December 2014 the student first shown the "hate fuck" poll (identified as student A in official documents)[5] showed it to senior administration in the student affairs office with a view to lodging a complaint under Dalhousie's Code of Student Conduct. She had also shown the screenshot to some of her female classmates, and they joined her in meeting with an administrator in the dentistry faculty to express their concern about the culture and climate in the school.

Within hours, university security identified nine men and five women from the screenshot. A student-in-crisis team was put together to determine if there was a safety risk and concluded there was not. The student affairs administrator then informed student A that there was no basis for an interim suspension of the men identified in the screenshot and, the next day, advised four of the women that the university's sexual harassment policy was the appropriate avenue in which to address their concerns. She referred them to the university's Human Rights, Equity and Harassment Prevention Office to pursue further recourse. University administration asked the dental school to provide support to the female students.

On 12 December student A met with members of the human rights office in the presence of a campus security officer and a female administrator from dentistry. She was informed of the formal and informal procedures available to her, and she opted for the formal ones to address her complaint. She asked for a "no contact order" with respect to three of her male classmates, and the campus security officer agreed. He also said that it would be helpful to obtain other evidence if there was any. Student A did not want to reveal the identity of her informant but, with his assistance, took fifty-four additional screenshots and gave them to university staff.

No-contact orders were served on the male students, and it was arranged for student A to write her December examinations in a room separate from her classmates. These measures meant that her complaint was now known to others, and student A began to experience the alienation that can be visited upon those who come forward in comparable circumstances. On 15 December human rights office staff offered to meet again with her and she declined, on account of exam pressures, emotional stress now aggravated by the fact that she had been identified as a complainant, and discomfort about another meeting with human rights personnel at this time. She wanted the university to launch an investigation under the Code of Student Conduct and retained a lawyer to advise her on matters going forward.

On the same day the story began to spread. The screenshots were obtained by CBC, and media stories began to appear and multiply, and pressure on dental students and on the university became intense. Dalhousie president Richard Florizone announced that he would take forty-eight hours to consider the allegations and began an intense round of discussions with colleagues, advisors, and some of the ten female students identified in the posts. An online petition to expel the Facebook group members had 50,000 signatures within weeks, and another 45,000 signed a petition calling for a transparent and independent investigation. The Nova Scotia Government announced that it was closely monitoring the situation. By now, the names of the thirteen members of the Facebook group were known to university authorities, and there was pressure from third parties and on social media to identify them. The university declined to do so on account of privacy.

Dissenting voices were heard too. Some downplayed the seriousness of the situation and thought the Facebook content no worse than that found on general Internet sites. Others cited privacy as a mitigating factor and denounced calls to expel the offenders as excessive.

The university administration's response to the scandal became apparent before the Christmas break. On 16 December, human rights office staff met with four female students named in the posts and with twelve of the thirteen Facebook group members (neither student A nor her informant was among their numbers, though the latter met separately with staff). On the next day, Florizone announced that the restorative justice option was favoured by a number of the women but did not close the door for them or others to pursue a formal complaint. He had decided not to initiate the formal investigation himself, though he emphasized that no options were foreclosed to the university by proceeding with restorative justice.

On 18 December, student A's informant – student B – apologized to his class and to the university president in a letter subsequently published in the press.[6] He stated that he had not been directly involved in the hurtful comments but that he would regret his membership in the Facebook group for the rest of his life. Meanwhile, remaining fourth-year dental exams were postponed until January, and most of the university paused for the Christmas holiday.

At about this time, a number of Dalhousie professors became more engaged in unfolding events. Eight of them met with Florizone on 17 December and were not satisfied by the meeting. They were concerned about the president's announcement of restorative justice and on 19 December posted a statement against misogyny and sexual violence on the Internet that attracted the signatures of 300 faculty and staff members. Four professors filed a complaint under the Code of Student Conduct describing the posts as sexual harassment and threats of sexual assault, and requested an investigation and suspension of students who had participated in the posts. They initially asked that their identities be kept confidential but, on 4 January, made their names and their complaint public. The Association of Nova Scotia University Teachers, a member of the Canadian Association of University Teachers, applauded the four, and they were supported by four female students in the class of 2015 who stated that "no individual woman in our class should be required to advance a formal complaint in her own name, or to participate as a witness. The University has enough information to initiate an investigation and move forward."[7]

Upon the resumption of classes in the new year, Florizone announced a suspension of clinic privileges of the thirteen Facebook

group members based on the dental clinic assistant dean's finding of unprofessionalism, and concerns for the safety of patients
and clinic staff. The interim suspension was confirmed by the
Faculty of Dentistry's academic standards class committee, which
indicated that it would consider violations of professionalism requirements in determining the duration of the suspensions and
possible remediation.

On 6 January, the Dalhousie Student Union and a social media
group, Anonymous, held a rally on campus that further provoked
concerns that restorative justice was not appropriate in this case. The
same day, four women in the class of 2015 published an open letter
calling upon the president to accept the formal complaint of the four
faculty members under the Code of Student Conduct. However,
the process called for a decision of the vice-president of student
affairs and, on 7 January, she decided not to accept the complaint
on the grounds that the code did not apply when a matter is before
a faculty as a failure to meet professional conduct requirements.

By 9 January students in the dentistry class of 2015 had returned
consent forms on their willingness to participate in restorative justice. Twelve of thirteen of the Facebook posters, and seventeen of
their classmates, fourteen of whom were women, including six of
nine women identified in the Facebook posts, said yes. The president spoke at a press conference: "This past month has been especially challenging for our university and our community. All of us
continue to be shaken by the misogynistic and completely unacceptable comments made by members of our fourth year dentistry
class … From the outset we stated that this behaviour is completely unacceptable and that there must be consequences. The consequences must be based on a just process that complies with the
law, university policy and the rights of those involved. We won't
rush to judgment nor will we sweep this under the rug."[8]

This did not satisfy the critics, and the local newspaper observed
that the suspensions, combined with the promise of restorative justice, "just seemed to fan the fury in many quarters."[9]

For the university, the path ahead was now clear. In addition to
the restorative justice initiative, there would be a three-person task
force on misogyny, sexism, and homophobia at Dalhousie, and a

strategic initiative on diversity and inclusion led by the university's law dean. In addition, the matter remained in front of the Faculty of Dentistry's academic standards committee charged with determining the professionalism issues.

In assessing the merits of alternative pathways, it is appropriate that we reflect upon a likely chain of events had the complaint of the four professors been accepted and the matter addressed through investigation and possible disciplinary action under the Code of Student Conduct. It is practically impossible for restorative justice and disciplinary processes to proceed in parallel. The former is about recognition, taking responsibility, repair, and hopefully reconciliation. The latter more closely mirrors the criminal justice process and is about denunciation and punishment. Where discipline is pursued, the focus of those threatened with punishment as severe as expulsion would have been exclusively on saving their professional lives, and they would have been well advised to say and do nothing in any other context that might diminish or compromise that focus. Any possibility for restorative justice would have been deferred, if not cancelled.

And the battle would be on. Facing potentially grave consequences, the Facebook members and their families would have retained lawyers. Presumably there were different degrees of participation in the posts: some members more active than others; some more provocative than others; perhaps others who encouraged posts but did not make them; still others only observers. This creates the potential for antagonistic defences and therefore a likelihood of separate representation for each of the (now) defendants. As many as thirteen lawyers for the defence would be joined by advocates for the university and, possibly if not likely, for some of the female students as well.

If the investigation led to a hearing, it likely would have been a public one. Although Dalhousie's Code prescribes an in camera hearing,[10] there would be applications by some of the lawyers to make it public in the interests of natural justice and transparency: justice must not only be done; it must be seen to be done. It would be difficult for the tribunal – the Senate Discipline Committee – to resist an application to convene in public, with the consequences that come with it, including the public disclosure of the names of the Facebook posters and those named in their posts. Even if the hearing was in camera, this would have been a likely consequence.

We should reflect, too, on the difficulty of a lay body like the Senate Discipline Committee presiding over a hearing of this kind. The judiciary in our criminal courts are knowledgeable and experienced in conducting hearings, including complicated ones involving several counsel. It is a fair bet that a committee of Dalhousie University senators would never have experienced a hearing as difficult as this one would have been. They, too, might have retained counsel to advise them on procedures and the rulings they might have to make.

This would take time. Investigation and a discipline hearing would have taken several months to conclude and it would have dominated the lives of all who had a major stake in the outcome. The detrimental impact on their academic progress would have been great, not to mention the emotional toll on them, and on their families and friends.

Perhaps above all, we must acknowledge that the issues in a disciplinary hearing are different, and narrower, than issues in restorative justice. They are focused on the charges, defences, and range of consequences, not on understanding, recognition, acceptance, and redress. They are focused on the defendants, not on those hurt by them: guilty or not guilty, and if the former, what should be their punishment?

Then there are the defences, and the arguments are foreseeable. One we could anticipate is that this matter was none of Dalhousie University's business. This was a Facebook group, not a campus club. Its members expected confidential communications among themselves, and as long as they did not break the law or university regulations, they should have been beyond the university's disciplinary reach. Dalhousie does not stand in loco parentis[11] to them, overseeing the appropriateness or morality of their behaviour. Once the decision not to lay criminal charges was made, the university should have stayed its hand as well.

The second and related defence would be based on privacy. It was an expectation of Facebook members that their communications were and would be private, and again – if not illegal – should not be subject to sanction: the state has no business in the bedrooms – or private chat rooms – of the nation.[12]

Another argument we might expect to hear is that the four faculty members did not have standing to make their complaint.[13] True, Dalhousie's Code of Student Conduct provides that anyone may make a complaint, but the argument would be that this means anyone with a sufficient interest may complain. Standing is a legal concept that requires a significant connection to the harm caused in order for someone to be a party to an action arising from it. The four faculty members were not among the victims of the Facebook group – so the argument goes – and they do not have standing to be complainants.

There would be individual defences too, arising from the nature and extent of each member's engagement in the Facebook group. Here their differences would be highlighted with potential conflicts among them about who did what and when. Whose idea was it? Who started it? What discussions were there apart from what might appear on the posts? Were there some who were observers or only minor participants? These and similar questions would be explored in mitigation of responsibility and punishment.

The point here is not whether these defences would prevail or be compelling – there are substantive arguments to the contrary. And once the activities of the Facebook group members became known outside their circle, whether intended or not, their behaviour became the business of the university. The point is that the issues in the case would have been argued, heard, and determined in the context of a discipline hearing. It would have been a long and painful ordeal, and the question is fairly asked: what would the process have done to address the harm caused by the Facebook group members to their female classmates, the Faculty of Dentistry, and to the broader university community? The answer is very little, if anything.

There remain two issues before we return to the restorative justice initiative at Dalhousie: first, the names of the Facebook group members and Dalhousie's decision not to release them for privacy reasons. There were many who sought to identify them by names,

whether for curiosity, prurient interest, ritualistic public denunciation, or, in the case of police and professional bodies, a desire to
advance their criminal investigations or to determine implications
for professional standing.

It is not unusual for university leaders to be asked to release
names of their students. A prospective employer may ask the dean
of engineering or of business for the names of top students in order
to get an upper hand in recruiting them. A law firm may ask the
law dean to name excellent prospects for summer employment to
get an early look at potential articling students. Another university may want to identify prospects for graduate education. Or as
here, investigative bodies may want names to advance their well-
understood purposes. Universities are constrained not only by
their own internal policies, but by law. In the case of Nova Scotia,
that law is the Freedom of Information and Protection of Privacy
Act, which states, "The head of a public body shall refuse to disclose information to an applicant if the disclosure would be an unreasonable invasion of a third person's personal privacy."[14]

In general, universities have good reason to refuse to disclose
names without the consent of those involved. Of course there are
exceptions, and there is room for disagreement about the scope of
those exceptions. But the starting point is no disclosure, and there
is potential liability if that prohibition is violated. In the Dalhousie
case, the police did not identify potential criminal infractions by
the Facebook group members, and the dentistry profession deferred its interest to the time at which they sought admission to its
ranks.[15] The university wisely resisted the entreaties to name the
group's members.

The second and larger issue was the reluctance or refusal of
those named in the Facebook posts to initiate the complaint under the Code of Student Conduct. We have seen that six of nine
supported the restorative justice initiative, but what about the
others? Why did they not launch the complaint? Their refusal
or reluctance to do so may be attributable to one or more factors: a desire to remain anonymous; the stigma associated with
sexual offences or transgressions; or a reluctance to prosecute a
transgression against colleagues, a supervisor, family member, or

friend. The issue is generic to sexual offences and is the main reason why they are under-reported and under-prosecuted.[16]

Canadian universities have been criticized for falling short
in making it easier for victims to come forward.[17] Most of them
still lack stand-alone policies for sexual assaults, though they are
under development at many institutions. The McGill University
policy on sexual violence is an example of the new approaches.
It proclaims a commitment "to creating and sustaining a safe environment through proactive, visible, accessible and effective approaches that seek to prevent and respond to sexual violence"[18]
and sets out three objectives:

a. to seek to prevent sexual violence through education and other
   proactive efforts to create awareness about the nature and effects
   of sexual violence;
b. to support Survivors of sexual violence; and
c. to respond effectively to Disclosures and Reports of Sexual
   Violence.

Section 9 of the policy sets out twelve guidelines for the effective
response to disclosure and reports, two of which are:

d. preserve the Survivor's privacy and confidentiality whenever
   possible under the law and applicable university policies and
   procedures;
i. respect, insofar as possible and taking into account the university's
   institutional obligations, the Survivor's decision to refrain from
   making a report.

These objectives and guidelines will constitute helpful tests to
judge institutional responses to offences of sexual transgression at
McGill and other Canadian universities. But they do not address
the broader questions of non-assaultive sexual behaviours involving faculty and students. UBC professor Steven Galloway's admission to a two-year-long affair with a student raises that question,
and in early 2016, UBC president Martha Piper advanced the idea

of a ban on romantic relations between professors and students.[19] She was not aware of any Canadian university that had imposed such a ban and she mused about whether its time had come. The idea was neither endorsed nor ruled out at her own university, but it was quickly rejected by the Canadian Association of University Teachers.[20] Leading American universities have been faster on the uptake. In 1997 Yale University banned all sexual relations between faculty and students, both undergraduate and graduate.[21] In 2015 Harvard University banned romantic and sexual relationships between professors and undergraduate students.[22] Northwestern University has a code on the subject[23] that bans romantic, dating, or sexual relations between faculty members or coaches and undergraduate students. It also provides for the removal of faculty from supervisory or evaluative authority in other circumstances.

We can expect closer attention to this issue by Canadian universities in coming years. But for now, we return to the Dalhousie story, where we have seen that there was opposition within the university to proceed with restorative justice. Concern was not limited to the university. Although Nova Scotia had been a provincial leader in the field,[24] "women's organizations objected that this was dangerous in cases of sexual assault and intimate partner violence and that it re-victimized women ... They convinced the province to place a Nova Scotia–wide moratorium on RJ for such cases. When RJ appeared to have been resurrected in the Facebook controversy, many feared that this was the thin edge of the wedge, and that it would lead to reintroducing RJ into criminal cases involving sexual violence."[25]

Opposition to the process did not end as restorative justice was launched and progressed. "During this period, and for much of February and March, the restorative justice process worked under constant threat that risked it being undermined or abandoned. These threats included error-filled press reports and aggressive media harassment of students ... Other threats included public denouncements of the process by non–Faculty of Dentistry professors and the Dalhousie Student Union; failed efforts by some professors to quash the restorative process at the Dalhousie University

Senate; threats of violence received against DDS2015 men via social media; and online harassment of female participants in restorative justice."[26]

But the process continued and would do so until late May. Its comprehensiveness and intensity is described in a detailed report prepared by its facilitators: law professor Jennifer Llewellyn, Dalhousie community safety officer Jacob MacIsaac, and Melissa MacKay, an advisor in harassment prevention and conflict resolution in Dalhousie's human rights office.[27] They were assisted by an advisory group of leading national and international experts in restorative justice, sexualized violence, and campus safety. The report refers to the misconception that restorative justice processes "are focused exclusively on bringing those individuals harmed together with those individuals who caused the harm in order to agree upon a 'settlement' to repair or heal the situation."[28]

> While this is how some restorative justice processes may be used, this is not the case for all restorative justice processes and not true for the restorative process at Dalhousie ... [The process here] was comprehensive in its focus. It examined the particular Facebook incident and its context and causes including systemic and cultural factors. It proceeded with particular attention to the needs of those harmed to ensure a trauma-informed process. [It] sought to understand the consequences and impacts of the incident and who was responsible, not in order to lay blame or impose punishment, but to determine what was required of the parties to respond to the harms, ensure action to prevent reoccurrence, and make positive changes in climate and culture for the future.[29]

We should leave to the participants the task of conveying the impact of this process. For the Faculty of Dentistry, restorative justice "was inclusive; it empowered students, staff and faculty alike to be part of the process ... [It] has shown us some of the next steps required and provided some of the skills and tools we will need to build a more inclusive and supportive learning and working environment."[30] For the university as a whole, restorative justice "has been inclusive and collaborative; focused on reflection, understanding and growth; precisely what a university should be."[31]

For the Nova Scotia Dental Association, the process "gave us both the ability to communicate impacts on the dental community ... and what we as the representatives of organized dentistry need to do to better serve the next generation of practicing dentists."[32] For the local advisory committee (professionals in various disciplines committed to restorative justice work), the process at Dalhousie "may well form a template for other institutions to address similar issues, not if, but when, they occur."[33]

From participants in the dentistry class of 2015: "As we reflect upon our five-month journey, we recognize how far we have come not only individually but collectively. We have challenged and supported one another as we confronted what happened with Facebook and the climate and culture within our school. These uncomfortable, difficult, and complicated conversations have required us to delve deeper into societal and cultural issues of sexism, homophobia, and discrimination and how they erode the foundations of supportive and healthy communities."[34]

For the female participants: "Restorative justice provided us with a different sort of justice than the punitive type most of the loudest voices seemed to want ... [W]e were not looking to have our classmates expelled as 13 angry men who understood no more than they did the day the posts were uncovered. Nor did we want simply to forgive and forget. Rather, we were looking for a resolution that would allow us to graduate alongside men who understood the harms they caused, owned these harms, and would carry with them a responsibility to do better."[35]

And for the members of the Facebook group:

> From the earliest moments of the restorative justice process when we realized the hurt and harm our comments caused for our classmates, faculty and staff we wanted to convey our overwhelming regret. But we learned that saying sorry is too easy. Being sorry, we have come to see, is much harder. It takes a commitment to hear and learn about the effects of your actions and an ongoing and lasting commitment to act differently in the future. We have hurt many of those closest to us. We do not ask for our actions to be excused. They are not excusable. We do commit to doing better as professionals, employers, alumni and friends.[36]

As the restorative justice process advanced, the Facebook group members were restored to clinics from which they had been suspended on 5 January, and the class of 2015 graduated on schedule in the spring.

What observations and conclusions are to be drawn from this Dalhousie University story? We must point, first, to the contrast between what actually happened and the potential unfolding of events had the complaint of the four professors proceeded to investigation and hearing under the Code of Student Conduct. The comparison above speaks for itself, and decisively in favour of restorative justice in this case, though some of its features require further comment.

One side of the story is speculative. We don't know what would have happened had there been a discipline hearing, and that is notable in itself. Once the matter is remitted to a hearing committee, it is in a space apart from the university commons, and that is how it must be when student defendants face potential academic capital punishment in the form of expulsion. The focus must be on fair process, the right to full answer and defence, and a penalty appropriate to the circumstances. Lawyers for the parties would have ensured this focus, and it would have excluded the four professors who made the complaint and whose standing to do so was tenuous; the student union leaders who supported them; the members of the class of 2015 other than in a capacity as witnesses; the rest of the Faculty of Dentistry, the university, and the profession. Discipline would have been an exclusionary process, and it would have excluded much of what was most important to bring closure to the dentistry class of 2015, to the rest of the university, and beyond.

And yet there was considerable pressure to go down this road. The first reaction of many in the midst of scandal or public controversy is a rush to get out in front of the issues, to be on the right side of those issues (and to establish their side as right), and to pressure leaders to declare themselves immediately, and take decisive action quickly. Certainly leadership must move with dispatch to ensure that supports are in place for victims, but a more deliberate approach is called for in determining the appropriate response to the transgressions. In this case, the president announced on 15 December that he was going to take forty-eight hours to weigh issues and alternatives. Considering that the clamour at the time within some university circles and in the social media was for stern discipline to be meted out to the Facebook group as quickly as possible, he was wise to do so. And yet, even when he made his decision in support of restorative justice, his critics struggled to overturn it, and some fought to undermine the process itself. There are many voices – and agendas – in the university commons, and finality does not come easily.

Some of these voices need to be reminded of the connection between authority and responsibility. "Whose neck is on the line?" is an important question. The necks of the four faculty members who pressed for disciplinary action under the Code of Student Conduct were not on the line; nor were those of the leadership of the Dalhousie Student Union or the many other protesting voices on campus or in the social media. But the neck of the university president was most assuredly on the line. A higher number of presidents of the ninety-six degree-granting institutions in Canada have been fired in the past fifteen years than have been the number of tenured faculty fired over the same period from among more than sixty thousand in our degree-granting universities and colleges.[37]

We are not privy to the deliberations of Dalhousie's Board of Governors, but it is reasonable to expect that the board – comprising faculty, staff, and students, along with public members – was closely attentive to the winds of change on campus and in the community over the Facebook affair, and that its different members reflected those shifting winds. If the decision on how to address the affair had turned out badly, the president would have paid a high price. University presidents are judged by results, though a gap between their responsibility and formal authority sometimes makes it difficult to produce results that are widely accepted on campus. Even after committing to restorative justice, Florizone was faced with attempts to undermine his decision by some faculty, student leaders, others on and off campus, and in social media. Within the board, too, his leadership may have hung in the balance until the success of restorative justice was apparent. Perhaps board members and president alike were relieved and even pleased when two of North America's most prominent media voices supported the approach that had been taken.[38] As noted by one of them, "Those found responsible for the online comments must show remorse, accept reasonable punitive consequences and apologize. If that happens, Dr Florizone will have taken an ugly moment and turned it into a teachable moment. We call that education."[39]

chapter three

Safe Space, Comfort, and Freedom of Expression: Stories from across Canada

Tolerance is one of the most familiar words in the English language. By definition it is neither virtue nor vice and may be either, depending on context. Its subject matter is usually negative; we don't tolerate things we like – we endorse or affirm them. We tolerate things we do not like but that we know we must not suppress or prohibit.

In our private lives, our tolerances may be closely aligned with our likes and dislikes. In our public lives, they must be informed by normative rules and values that frame our social order. Fundamental among these is freedom of expression, described by chief justice Beverley McLachlin as "the indispensable condition of nearly every other freedom."[1] "Not only is the guarantee of central concern to free and democratic societies, it potentially is broad enough to cover all variety of activities. If the guarantee traditionally has been linked to political freedom, freedom of expression has expanded well beyond its roots in democracy to encompass nearly all non-violent forms of expression."[2]

Freedom of expression is also an "indispensable condition" of the university commons, though it has been tested so often in recent years that it is not hyperbole to describe our commons as a contemporary battleground over its boundaries. At Concordia University the once and future prime minister of Israel was silenced by protesters; and at the University of Ottawa, a scheduled speech by a controversial American commentator was cancelled because of safety concerns. At the University of Calgary, anti-abortion demonstrators were subject to non-academic discipline and legal charges. At Brock, University of Toronto, and Queen's, Halloween costumes touched off racism controversies. At York University, a mural depicting a Palestinian protest was at the centre of a controversy involving a donor. Campaigns to link Israel's policies on Palestine with apartheid in South Africa generated controversies on more than one campus. A yoga instructor's free class at the University of Ottawa was cancelled upon encountering resistance from student leaders alleging cultural misappropriation. A Laurentian University professor was removed from a course for asking students to sign a waiver agreeing to transfer to another section of the same course if they found his use of bad language in class to be offensive or uncomfortable. A University of Toronto professor was told that he must use genderless pronouns. A Ryerson professor and School of Social Work director was accused of "a violent act of anti-Blackness, misogyny and misogynoir" when he left an anti-racism meeting on campus. Most recently, the director of McGill University's Institute for the Study of Canada resigned in the wake of controversy precipitated by an article he wrote for *Maclean's* magazine.

Members of the general public who hear of these controversies might well ask, "What on earth is going on in our universities?" Those within them would be wise to ask the same question. Are these examples of tensions that must play out in the interests of inclusion? Or are they behaviours that diminish our commons and threaten its vitality? To answer the question we must consider the examples themselves, both individually and cumulatively.

Free Speech at Concordia and University of Ottawa

Concordia University had agreed to host Benjamin Netanyahu when he arrived to speak there on 9 September 2002. He was prevented from doing so when pro-Palestinian demonstrators rioted with a fervour that led the university to cancel his speech and to ban events relating to the Israeli-Palestinian conflict for one month. A decade later, at the University of Ottawa, writer and commentator Ann Coulter's scheduled speech was cancelled following "boisterous demonstrations outside that sponsors of the appearance feared could turn violent."[3] There was a common theme to reasons given for the demonstrations as articulated by some of their participants. "There's no free speech for hate speech," said one of them at Concordia.[4] "We don't tolerate hate speech," said another at the University of Ottawa.[5] Also at U of O, the university's provost had anticipated possible infractions of the country's hate laws by Coulter and wrote to her in advance of her scheduled talk warning her to conform to what is legally acceptable in Canada.[6]

Whether or not Canada's hate code provisions are threatened or violated is determined by the criminal justice system. The laws themselves challenge the principle that we should know in advance behaviours that will attract criminal liability, and their enforcement has been difficult because the boundaries between severe criticism, condemnation even, and hate speech are not clear. The best test relies on the intent of the speaker: is there or was there an intention to promote hatred against an identifiable group? None of this could be determined by the demonstrators or by the University of Ottawa provost, and the demonstrations should be seen for what they were: attempts to shut down speakers whose speeches were never heard but were anticipated to be offensive to the demonstrators. This is objectionable in any setting and deeply troubling in universities.

In the domain of free speech these two episodes are what we might colloquially call no-brainers. But that should not lead us to dismiss them as aberrations a decade apart in time, and isolated examples that illustrate the normal tolerance for free speech on campus. Their most enduring consequences may be unmeasurable and may lie in their reinforcement of conformity both in topics addressed and voices heard in the commons. We have seen, at Concordia, that following the cancellation of Netanyahu's speech there was a one-month ban on events relating to the Israeli-Palestinian conflict. We should worry about any such ban, but additionally we must ask whether it lasted officially for one month and unofficially for much longer, thereby effectively foreclosing debate for a long time on an issue of global significance on a university campus.

There is an additional and related topic raised by these examples. "By allowing [Ann Coulter] on campus, it has created an unsafe space," said one of the organizers of the Ottawa protest.[7] This idea of safe space will recur throughout this chapter, so it merits our attention now. Current use suggests two different meanings. The first is an idea rooted in the experience of identifiable groups or minorities that people who have experienced the trauma of discrimination need an opportunity – a safe space – in which to come together to share their experiences without fear of harassment, criticism, or judgment. The idea is intended to legitimize perspectives because they are held, and to reinforce positive self-images in the face of experiences that may have had the opposite effect.

There can be no objection to this idea if the assembly has been organized by people of similar interest or experience and is for their attendance and participation. It is akin to a private gathering of any kind, except for the fact that universities need to be accommodating to the need for safe space as so defined. The problem arises (and the second definition emerges) when it is argued that the safe space must extend outward and into the public domain, along with its protections against interference or intrusion from those who hold different views or whose ways of expressing them may cause unease. It is in this sense that safe space claims may conflict with free speech, and it is this sphere that the University of Chicago's dean of students had in mind when he wrote in 2016 to the incoming class of 2020,

> Once here you will find that one of the University of Chicago's defining characteristics is our commitment to freedom of inquiry and expression … Members of our community are encouraged to speak, write, listen, challenge and learn, without fear of censorship. Civility and mutual respect are important to all of us, and freedom of expression does not mean the freedom to harass or threaten others. You will find that we expect members of our community to be engaged in rigorous debate, discussion and even disagreement. At times this may challenge you and even cause discomfort.
>
> Our commitment to academic freedom means that we do not support so-called "trigger warnings," we do not cancel invited speakers

because their topics might prove controversial, and we do not condone the creation of intellectual "safe spaces" where individuals can retreat from ideas and perspectives at odds with their own.[8]

If safety is construed in the first sense described above, and if in the public context it extends to physical safety combined with an expectation of civility and mutual respect, it is compatible with freedom of expression. Extending the meaning of safety more broadly (as in the claim that inviting Ann Coulter to the University of Ottawa threatened to create an unsafe space on campus) is incompatible with that freedom and a threat to the vitality of the commons.

Anti-Abortion Demonstrators at University of Calgary

For more than a decade, the University of Calgary Campus Pro-Life group has held on-campus demonstrations against abortion using posters of aborted fetuses and comparing abortion to genocide. The protests sparked counter-demonstrations and complaints to the university administration, which instructed the group to turn their posters inwards so that others would have a choice whether or not to view them. Campus Pro-Life refused and thereby precipitated warnings of legal action by the university followed by charges of non-academic misconduct, and trespassing charges that were later stayed (discontinued though potentially recurring).

The non-academic misconduct charges alleged that by failing to turn their posters inward or to leave campus when requested to do so, Campus Pro-Life demonstrators had committed a major violation of the non-academic misconduct policy. Major violations are those that "endanger the safety and/or security of another individual or the University of Calgary community" by, inter alia, failure to comply with a campus security officer or university official in the legitimate pursuit of his or her duties.[9] The charges were heard by the associate vice-provost of student success and learning support services, and findings of misconduct were registered against the students and formal written warnings were issued to them.

Two internal appeals followed: the first, to the internal appeal board, which declined to hear the appeal, and second, to the Board of Governors, which delegated its authority to hear the matter to the appeal board, which requires establishing whether there are grounds for the appeal before a hearing panel is convened. The chair of the committee ruled that grounds for the appeal were not established, and the students sought judicial review of this decision in the Court of Queen's Bench in Alberta.[10]

The case was heard by justice Karen Horner, and her thirty-five-page written decision was issued in April 2014. Much of her analysis focused on procedural matters that are not germane to present concerns, but her analysis of Charter issues is central to them because the Campus Pro-Life students argued that their Charter right to freedom of expression had been violated by the university. The judge's consideration of this subject did not rest on settled law. Section 32 tells us that the Charter applies (a) to the Parliament and Government of Canada in all matters within the authority of Parliament; and (b) to the legislature and government of each province in all matters within the authority of the legislature of each province.[11] At issue is whether "legislature and government" includes universities. In 1990, the Supreme Court of Canada held that the Charter did not apply to universities,[12] but in 1997 the Court held that it applies to entities that are controlled by government or to activities that are governmental, in the sense that they are carried on through implementation of a certain government program.[13] This opened the door to argument that because the provision of education is a government program, universities are not "Charter-free zones"[14] and the Pro-Life students have a Charter-protected right of freedom of expression.

Judge Horner's decision in this case will not put to rest all arguments about the application of the Charter to university activities. Her decision overturned the results of the internal appeal processes of the University of Calgary and directed its appeal committee to "convene as soon as reasonably practical to hear the Students' appeal" on grounds that included the Charter-protected freedom of expression argument.[15] It was clear from her reasoning that Justice Horner did not think much of the university's claim that its instructions to the Pro-Life students to turn their signs inward was the appropriate resolution of the conflict here: "The Appeal Board's consideration of the severity of the interference with the Students' Charter-protected interests is limited to the fact that the University did not ban the [Pro-Life] display, but rather requested the students to turn their signs inwards. Neither the Appeal Board's nor [its chairman's] decisions address the effect that this might have on the ability of the students to realistically express their thoughts and beliefs."[16]

Two conclusions emerge from the story of this dispute. First, a better resolution would have been to allow the Pro-Life students to demonstrate as they had been doing since 2005, and to have security personnel nearby to keep the peace – should that prove necessary – for the two days in each term that the display was mounted.[17] Those who did not wish to view the posters needed only to look elsewhere. Second, and more generally, we can expect Charter rights and values to be raised more often in disputes in the commons. This does not require quick and easy resort to lawyers and courts to solve issues that could not be settled in the commons. It does require disputants and university officials to internalize and take seriously the directions and guidance to which Charter rights and values point. It is called "taking rights seriously."[18]

Costume Parties at Brock, University of Toronto, and Queen's

Halloween is proving more controversial than once it was. In 2009 five University of Toronto students, dressed as Jamaica's bobsled team, won a prize at a Halloween event sponsored by three of the university's colleges. Five years later, four non-Black Brock University students did the same thing. And this year, Queen's University students attended an off-campus costume party wearing what were described as stereotypical national costumes.

All three episodes triggered racism controversies. In the case of the U of T and Brock students, the discussion centred on their use of blackface or make-up used by non-Black performers to portray

Black persons. Its use has a long history and one frequently, though not always, viewed as racist. Here the students were not portraying Black persons in stereotypical, oppressed, or disadvantaged situations. Nor is it likely that they were paying tribute to the participation of a tropical team in a winter Olympic sport that inspired the movie *Cool Runnings*.[19] It was their use of blackface that ignited the controversy.

The University of Toronto Black Students Association compared the costumes and make-up to the wearing of Nazi regalia,[20] and the organization demanded apologies from the three colleges that sponsored the event. U of T drama and English professor Stephen Johnson, who has researched the performance of race on North American and British stages remarked, "If you asked 50 different people [about the costumes], they'll all see 50 different things."[21] The students who dressed as the bobsled team "said they didn't intend to offend anyone and were trying to portray the characters in the movie *Cool Runnings*."[22] "This movie played a large part in our childhoods and we simply wanted to express our feelings towards it with realistic costumes, which in this case included skin colour."[23] They nevertheless apologized at a town hall meeting held by the university to discuss the event.

Five years later, the episode at Brock was received in similar fashion. Faculty and a student in the university's labour studies program described the students who dressed up as the bobsled team members as "racist, full stop."[24] The Brock University Students' Union indicated that a union representative would be present at future costume parties to vet costumes at the door.

At Queen's, mostly white students wore costumes depicting themselves as sheiks, guerrillas from the war in Vietnam, Buddhist monks, Mexicans, and other national or ethnic peoples. The costumes were described as inappropriate by the student government, and the party fuelled a demonstration at the university the purpose of which was outlined by the media spokesperson for the protesters: "We want there to be set in place clear consequences and accountability for the racist actions that were actually undertaken by the students and actually enforcing them."[25] This was part of a wider agenda that included "mandatory training on issues of oppression for staff and faculty at Queen's; mandatory training for all counsellors working at Student Wellness Services on how to deal with racism and other issues; creating a mandatory course for incoming students, [and] educating them in indigenous issues and race issues."[26]

If there was insensitivity to issues of race in the selection of costumes by party-goers at the three universities, there was also a lack of proportion in the responses to them. These were Halloween parties, not cultural misappropriations, Nazi mimicry, or manifestations of disapproval of other peoples. So describing them risks diminishing real problems of intolerance, discrimination, and racism. It also risks backlash from a bewildered public observing these episodes. No country in the world has adapted to multiculturalism more successfully than has Canada; most Canadians know that and appreciate our diversity. They would also remind us that the episodes described here were just Halloween parties.

Israel/Palestine

No contemporary issue has galvanized more attention on university campuses in Canada and abroad than has the relationship between Israel and Palestine. In early 2016 Paul Bronfman discontinued his financial and other support of York University on account of a mural in the university's student centre that he felt represented hatred towards the Jewish people. The mural had won a student art prize and showed a young Palestinian man poised to throw rocks at a bulldozer in the distance, presumably representing Israeli construction in the West Bank. Mr Bronfman was not alone in his concern. The president of the Friends of the Simon Wiesenthal Centre for Holocaust Studies described the mural as "inciting hate against Israel, it's inciting violence."[27] Another student described the mural as "symptomatic of a toxic campus climate against Jewish students."[28]

Of wider concern to many people is the Israeli Apartheid movement. The equation of Israel's policies towards Palestinians with the treatment of South African Blacks under apartheid has attracted support from several student unions and from the Canadian Federation of Students. The movement's Israeli Apartheid Week and its companion BDS (Boycott, Divestment, and Sanctions) campaign against Israel has led to pressure on universities to break ties with the country and its universities.

There are two levels on which we must consider the issues here, and the first is the easier one. It requires that universities honour freedom of expression, and that means the mural in the Student Centre stays there until those responsible decide otherwise, and that critics of Israeli policies are free to describe their views as they see fit, including the equation of those policies with apartheid. The meaning of the mural is for its beholders to interpret and discuss; and whether the claim that Israeli policy amounts to apartheid is ahistorical and unjust – as this writer believes it is – or well founded is a matter for debate.

The second level for our consideration rests on a recognition that militancy is an enemy of debate. Militant supporters of a cause don't seek debate; they have reached their conclusions and seek action, and they are not averse to employing threats and intimidation to have their way. Militancy has been observable in the Israeli-Apartheid movement, and it was manifested in the demonstrations that turned into riots at Concordia and the University of Ottawa. Universities must do a better job of confronting and countering militancy, and that includes taking disciplinary action in appropriate cases. It is telling that in our consideration of student behaviours to date, the only disciplinary process carried through to a conclusion involved the Pro-Life group at the University of Calgary and theirs was demonstrative, though reportedly not militant. The militancy and destructiveness of the Concordia and University of Ottawa students went unpunished.[29]

There is a message here, too, for student unions. They are representative organizations, and they represent all their members on the theory that their mandates relate to student life and programs, and relations between students and their universities. When they extend their activities beyond student interests and into a wider political domain, and ally themselves with protagonists in that realm, they are not representing all of their members; indeed they may be at odds with some or many of them. Jewish students at York, or anywhere else where their union has joined the Israeli-Apartheid movement, should seek recourse through their university and provincial governments – legislated recourse if necessary – to allow them to withdraw from the union and have their membership fees returned to them.

We can imagine the repercussions if the York University Students' Union joined Christians United for Israel. It would produce a revolt within their members and a splintering of the membership with representations to the university and government to amend membership rules. There is no difference in principle with the present case. Students should not be required to be members of an organization that extends its activities into the political realm and attaches itself to ideologies or values with which they are at odds. And students themselves, with the assistance of their universities' leadership, and governments (where legislative change may be required) should put an end to it.

Yoga Instruction at University of Ottawa

In September 2015 a yoga instructor who had been teaching a free class for the university's Centre for Students with Disabilities was advised that her course was discontinued. It was not discontinued for the usual reasons courses are cancelled: low student numbers, outdated content, shortcomings in instruction, or financial contingencies. According to a representative of the University of Ottawa's Student Federation, "Yoga has been under a lot of controversy lately due to how it is being practiced and what practices from what cultures (which are often sacred spiritual practices) they are being taken from. Many of these cultures are cultures that have experienced oppression, cultural genocide and diasporas due to colonialism and western supremacy, and we need to be mindful of this and how we express ourselves ... while practicing yoga."[30]

This may come as a surprise to the United Nations, whose General Assembly in 2014 designated 21 June as International Day of

Yoga. The day was first observed worldwide a few months before the Ottawa class was cancelled. It may also come as a surprise to the students with disabilities for whom yoga brings some relief to find themselves associated in this way with oppression.

Misappropriation of the identity of another may occur as a result of theft, violation of intellectual property rights, imitation, or reproduction without permission. Cultural misappropriation may occur when what is stolen, confiscated, borrowed, imitated, or reproduced is in substance or symbol the property of an identifiable population or group and held to be one of its defining or identifying features. An archetypical example is Aboriginal headdress. Wearing one is an earned right and carries spiritual and symbolic meaning. It is not a sartorial preference, and wearing it without having earned it is cultural misappropriation.

Identifying cultural misappropriation from among genuine cases, cultural exchanges or borrowings, flattering imitation, and historical practices that have evolved over millennia, is difficult work. In the case of yoga, we are dealing with a history originating in India and dating back almost three thousand years. Its theory and practice appears to have been introduced in the West by its Eastern practitioners, not encountered in the course of Western expansion or adventurism. At some point in a long history that has spread across the globe, a tradition once identified by its cultural roots enters the international public domain, and its practice is no longer either appropriation or misappropriation. There is a compelling argument that this is what has occurred with yoga.

Fortunately it was not long before the cancellation of the yoga class at University of Ottawa was reversed. In early 2016 the course was reinstated with a new instructor, a Canadian of Indian ancestry. But allegations of cultural appropriation will be heard again.

Correcting Professors at Laurentian, University of Toronto, and Ryerson

Michael Persinger is a cognitive neuroscientist and professor of psychology at Laurentian University. In December 2015 he was informed by the university's provost that he would not be continuing to teach his section of the university's year-long course in introductory psychology. At the beginning of term he had asked students assigned to his section to sign a statement of understanding headed "This Course is rated 'R' for coarse language and explicit content." It was an acknowledgment of his warning that he used profanity and other language they might find offensive in his class. He had used the warning for years, and the option for students disturbed by either the warning or his language in class was to register in another section of what is typically a large, multi-sectioned course taught by several professors.

There was, said Persinger, a pedagogical rationale for his approach. His language was intended to help his students approach disturbing language with critical thinking. "One of my techniques is to expose people to all types of different words, ... [s]illy words, complex words, emotional words, profane words. Because they influence how you make decisions and how you think."[31]

By using such words, he said, he can teach his students about their impact on the brain.[32] "One of the first things I say in the first lecture is one of the purposes of this course is to free you from being a victim of your own language ... I tell all my classes: You can ask any question you want, no matter how politically incorrect. You can use the words you want, no matter how inappropriate. We will then evaluate it step by step."[33]

He also said that he used "innuendo and ribald jokes" to keep his students' attention during his lectures.[34] Most professors would wish to attract their students' attention in ways that fall short of the measures employed by Persinger, but with a sea of desktop computers in front of him, and with frequent referencing of handheld devices, he might understandably have concluded that more than professorial erudition was necessary to engage them.

When the issue of academic freedom was raised, Laurentian's provost replied, "It's not about academic freedom ... It's simply that a faculty member cannot ask a student to sign a document or memorandum of understanding as a condition to take his or her class ... Admission requirements are set by senate."[35]

This story was also seen to raise the issue of what have become known as "trigger warnings" or advance warnings to students of course materials that might trigger difficult emotional responses in them. Depending on perspective, they are mollycoddling students, a violation of academic freedom or safety measures appropriate to a diverse student body.

Later in 2016 another psychology professor – the University of Toronto's Jordan Peterson – launched a YouTube video, "Fear and the Law," part 1 of his lecture series titled "Professor against Political Correctness." His subject was non-binary gender identities (an umbrella term for people who do not self-identify always as either male or female). He took issue with Bill C-16, introduced in the House of Commons in May 2016 to amend the Canadian Human Rights Act and the Criminal Code to achieve two goals: first, to add gender identity and gender expression to the list of prohibited grounds of discrimination; and second, to extend the protection of Criminal Code hate propaganda protection to persons with non-binary gender identities.

The gist of Peterson's lecture was that the legislation goes too far in accommodating non-binary and transgender people[36] and that its vagaries will lead to uncertainty and legal disputes. His views were rebutted by colleagues at the university and others, but it was the issue of language that brought him into conflict with the university administration. The pronouns *he* and *she* do not fit non-binary people who sometimes choose other pronouns by which they would prefer to be identified. *They/them/their, ze, hir,* and *zir* are among the possibilities. There may be grammatical errors or infelicities in their use, but that was not Peterson's main point. He said that if asked to refer to a particular student by a gender-neutral pronoun, he would not do so. "I don't recognize another person's right to determine what pronouns I use to address them. I won't do it."[37]

Peterson was cautioned by senior administrators, and cautioned again, not to use language that might be discriminatory under the law. They implicitly linked him causally to threats made against transgender students by referring to them in a letter: "We trust that these impacts on students and others were not your intention.

However in view of these impacts, as well as the requirements [of legislation], we urge you to stop repeating these statements."[38] Peterson indicated that he would not be deterred by the possibility that he might be prosecuted for a hate crime.[39]

The third example in our trilogy under this subheading occurred at Ryerson University on 27 October 2016. Henry Parada, director of the university's School of Social Work, left an anti-racism meeting at a time when, according to the Black Liberation Collective Ryerson branch, "Black folks were giving praise to a young Black woman professor at a critical and vulnerable time." This earned Parada a rebuke for "a violent act of anti-Blackness, misogyny, and misogynoir (a newish term for misogyny directed at Black women)."[40]

The following day the Black Liberation Collective sent Parada an open letter demanding his resignation. The letter said that his actions "perpetuate anti-black racism" and that he does not "value anti-black racism scholarship, black women, black educators or education, black experiences, black life and ultimately black students."[41]

On 16 November the dean of the Faculty of Community Services announced that Parada had stepped down as director. No reasons were given for his departure.

Our first observation about this trilogy is that we can expect to hear more about each of the examples. There is a grievance, and possibly an investigation, to come at Lakehead; Peterson's situation at U of T may turn on whether a formal complaint is made against him; and we know next to nothing about the context of Parada's resignation at Ryerson.

On the basis of what we do know, it would seem that Persinger's claim to academic freedom in the Lakehead example is a strong one. It is true, as the provost said, that admission requirements are not Persinger's responsibility, but this is not so much an admissions issue as it is access to another section in a multi-sectioned course. And that issue is being determined – not by Persinger himself – but by a student opting out of his class because of his use of language.

Administrators are often influenced by an idea reminiscent of Kant's categorical imperative, whether they know it by that source or not. It directs humans to act in accordance with the maxim that all in similar circumstances should act in the same way. This may translate for the provost into the question: what if everyone did as Persinger did? The answer is that everyone won't do as Persinger did (the categorical imperative is moral guidance, not a behavioural rule) and if they did so, the problem would be a different one that would require a different solution determinable if and when it occurred.

The more general issue of trigger warnings is raised by this example. The phrase "denotes a growing tendency among North American university student groups to demand that professors provide advance warning about course material – books, films, discussion topics that might produce anxiety, panic attacks, or post-traumatic stress disorder from students who have been victims of sexual abuse or assault, or who believe that they are the victims of systemic discrimination."[42]

While there have been some student initiatives in this direction, particularly in the United States, it is not a movement with traction. It should not become one. Course names, outlines, and syllabi inform students about subject matter and course materials. It may be that from time to time professors would be wise to caution one or more of their students about material that might be unexpected and that might cause anxiety for them. It is a matter best left to their professional judgment.

The Peterson example at the University of Toronto also raises issues of academic freedom. Should a complaint be made against him, it would be assessed against the university's Statement on Equity, Diversity and Excellence, the Ontario Human Rights Code, the requirements of academic freedom, and the Charter guarantee of freedom of expression. Peterson would have a formidable defence. While he should be reminded that his students' wishes to be identified in ways that respect their non-binary gender identities are as important to them as the manner of his speech is important to him, and that it would be reasonable for him to accede to their wishes in this respect, this is not a matter on which he can be told what to do.

In the case of Parada, the outburst of the Black Liberation Collective Ryerson Branch is inexplicable on the known facts. We do not know why Parada left the anti-racism meeting when he did: time pressures, health break, or an important cellphone call? Was he feeling unwell? Perhaps he found some of what was being said at the meeting distasteful. It is credible to suggest that this may be an example of an attempt to extend safe space from the private to the public domain, and in that sense comparable to the Concordia and University of Ottawa examples above. If the anti-racism event was a public one, people in attendance are free to leave when they wish, for any reason. Even if it was a private one, those present can choose the timing of their departures.

The Andrew Potter Essay in *Maclean's*

On 1 August 2016 philosopher-journalist Andrew Potter became director of McGill University's Institute for the Study of Canada. Less than eight months later he resigned from his "dream job" after an article he wrote in *Maclean's* magazine was critically received. The article is titled "How a Snowstorm Exposed Quebec's Real Problem: Social Malaise."[43] The storm stranded 300 vehicles on a major Montreal highway overnight on 14 March, and the circumstances led Potter to write that "Quebec is an almost pathologically alienated and low trust society, deficient in many of the most basic forms of social capital that other Canadians take for granted." He went on to comment on the debasement of police and emergency service uniforms by protesting members of both organizations, the large size of Quebec's underground economy, social isolation, low civic engagement, and lack of trust.

It was a provocative article in a well-known magazine, and one that predictably would be controversial. We might well ask, so what? This article, however, did not win favourable reviews in the premier's office or by his own employer. Premier Couillard described it as "an article of very low quality,"[44] and the university tweeted that Potter's views did not represent those of McGill. He had second thoughts about what he had written, issued a public apology, and resigned as director of the institute, citing "negative reaction from within the university community and the broader public" as the reason for his resignation.[45] He retained his professorship and will remain on faculty at the university.

The episode attracted immediate and widespread concern, including questions about the circumstances of the resignation. The university denied pressure from or contact with the premier's office, and responded to academic freedom concerns through the principal, who reported that Potter "recognized that he had failed to uphold ... [the institute's] mission and that the credibility of the institute would be best served by the resignation."[46]

There are several issues here and they begin with what we don't know. Did Potter resign of his own volition, or was his resignation requested by the institute's board of trustees or the university's administration? Was it embarrassment about his second thoughts about the article that led to his resignation, or was he compelled to step down? Answers to these questions would influence our response to yet another question: should the resignation have been accepted or refused by the university? These questions will persist until they are satisfactorily answered.

On the basis of what we do know, it is possible to debate whether Potter had the benefits of academic freedom, free speech, or both; and the constraints on that speech – if any – imposed by his administrative office. It is argued in this book that there are material differences between academic freedom and free speech that demand greater precision in determining which is in play in a particular context, and that administrative and governance offices may sometimes limit both freedoms.[47] In this case it appears that Potter's article was sufficiently connected to his academic duties that we must conclude that he was exercising his academic freedom.

Administrative office per se does not carry academic freedom with it, and so it is notable that Potter stepped away from his directorship but retains his professorship. If he felt that he had compromised effective leadership of the institute, or if those to whom he reported reached the same conclusion, his resignation is understandable, whether on his own initiative or with the encouragement of the administration. It is possible, in the exercise of one's academic freedom, to jeopardize the reputation of an institution one leads, in this case the institute.

But these considerations do not answer all our questions about this case. The university's tweet distancing McGill from Potter's article is troubling for two reasons: first, it tells us nothing we didn't know already; no one is going to conclude from the article that Potter is speaking for McGill University or for anyone but himself. In that sense the tweet was needless, though it was not harmless. It implied official criticism of his views by his employer, and for that reason alone it should have been avoided.

We should note that academic freedom does not shield anyone from criticism for its exercise; Potter could reasonably expect criticism for his article, including that from high offices. But his employer must be mindful that its public and official rebuke – in this case, in the name of the university itself – may discourage its exercise, whether by Potter or others in the future. University officials are perfectly entitled to express disagreement with Potter in private or in public, but they must be careful not to do so in a manner that might reasonably be taken to discourage the exercise of academic freedom. That test was not met in this case.

Conclusion

How do we answer the question of the hypothetical member of the general public referenced at the beginning of this chapter: what is going on at our universities? Do the above stories represent the normal machinations of institutions committed to the search for truth struggling with new realities? Are some of them illustrations of political correctness run rampant? There is no single answer, no one generalization that summarizes the collective. But there are themes to be drawn out from them, and for the writer the most important are two: first, freedom of expression is under attack in our universities – not a deliberate, organized attack, but an accumulation of episodes that diminish its significance in comparison to other considerations. Second, the concept of universities as intellectual spaces is also under attack as a result of intellectual laziness accompanied by ideology and anger. The result, too often, is not a contest of ideas; it is a struggle for power.

Students of free speech and expression will recall the example that one is not free to falsely shout "Fire!" in a crowded theatre. The example is important for two reasons. First it was discussed as a singular or rare exception, apart from what is proscribed by law, to a right to speak freely. Second, it informs us that, in general, freedom of expression is to be curbed only in anticipation of imminent and real harm. A false alarm of fire in a crowded theatre will send patrons stampeding to the exits, with the likelihood that some will suffer bodily harm and perhaps death. This danger is foreseeable, tangible, and imminent.

When we reflect upon the examples in this discussion, danger of this kind is not to be found. Two of them (Concordia and Ottawa) were militant and successful campaigns to silence invited guest speakers. Another (Calgary) was an attempt to force anti-abortion demonstrators to turn their placards inward, and thereby hinder them in conveying their messages to anyone other than themselves. Still another (U of O) saw a shutting down of a yoga class because its exercises and rituals were said to have been improperly removed from their cultural roots. Brock, U of T, and Queen's witnessed narrow interpretations of Halloween costumes and overreaction to them. York experienced a Jewish philanthropist seeking the removal of art he considered hate at a university at which Jewish students report silencing by a toxic campus environment. Still others feature speech correction (Laurentian, U of T) and strident denunciation of an academic program director for reasons inferred from his leaving a meeting (Ryerson).

Anyone who has worked for long at one or more of our universities will attest that these are examples of which there are more; they continue to accumulate at the time of writing.[48] They are not exceptional or unusual instances of attitudes and behaviours undermining freedom of expression on our campuses. This freedom is seen by many as one among competing values rather than the "indispensable condition of every other freedom" described by Chief Justice McLachlin.

The concept of universities as intellectual spaces has suffered too, though not only because of interference with freedom of expression. Intellectual work is hard work, and those committed to it must take the time to inform themselves carefully, to think their way through complicated questions, and to test their thinking in the marketplace of ideas. This requires disciplined, patient effort, and a determination to engage and listen to others. The path of less resistance is an easier path. It features emotion over intellect and denunciation instead of argument, and is aggravated by quick and ready access to publicity and organization through social media. Writers in the *Economist* were referring to the Trump campaign when they wrote, "There is a strong case that, in America and elsewhere, there is a shift towards the politics in which feelings trump facts more freely and with less resistance than used to be the case. Helped by new technology, a deluge of facts and a public much less given to trust than once it was, some politicians are getting away with a new depth and pervasiveness of falsehood. If this continues, the power of truth as a tool for solving society's problems could be lastingly reduced."[49]

These words have wider import. Rather than yielding to this shift, or being complicit in it, our universities should lead in the struggle against it. That struggle begins with a recommitment to freedom of expression as the first principle in their missions.

chapter four

Academic Freedom and Governance – A Reprise: Carleton's Blogging Board Member

Root Gorelick is a Carleton University biology professor who was elected to serve on the university's Board of Governors. He also authored a public blog on which he recorded a running and detailed commentary on board deliberations during its public meetings. The blog was critical, sometimes derisively so, of board decisions, other board members, and university administrators. Professor Gorelick vowed civil disobedience in response to the board's code of conduct enumerating the duties and responsibilities of board members, and upon refusing to sign it when seeking a second term, he was deemed ineligible to serve.

This, said Carleton University's faculty union, was a violation of Professor Gorelick's academic freedom. The Canadian Association of University Teachers agreed, denouncing the board's Code of Conduct and applauding Professor Gorelick's "principled decision to resist pressure to suppress his academic freedom and free speech rights."[1] Carleton's Graduate Students Association passed a motion supporting Gorelick's "principled efforts to make university decision-making more open and transparent."[2] Five other Carleton student and employee unions joined in and called for Carleton employees to have at least a 50 per cent plus 1 majority on the board.[3] CAUT's threatened censure of Carleton University remains outstanding.

We saw in chapter 1 that there are both similarities and differences between university boards and those of other organizations. They have similar oversight and financial responsibilities, but there are marked differences with respect to powers and composition: in universities, governance is shared and academic authority resides in a senate or equivalent body, and their boards are composed of university insiders as well as external members. In addition to the president and chancellor, Carleton's thirty-two-member board includes two faculty members, two representatives from the Senate, four students, two staff members, two alumni association nominees, and eighteen members of the general public.

Boards of governors are not well understood by the general university population. Among their burdens, the least understood is their role in protecting university independence. Without them, financial oversight of public universities would fall to government. Their financial statements would be consolidated with those of government and would be debated in the legislature and its committees, as they would be for those of government departments. The president's reporting line would likely be to a deputy minister of the government department responsible for post-secondary education, and that department might also have authority to hire, and if deemed necessary to fire, university presidents. Universities don't want this and, fortunately, our governments have not wanted it either, which is why they have provided for boards of governors or their equivalents in legislation or charters.

It is in this context that the respective numbers of insiders and external members matter most. Boards can protect university independence only if most of their members are from outside the university. They are appointed by government, or in the name of the public, to represent their interest and are the only arm's-length board members. All others hold university offices or represent internal university interests and, without a majority of externals, boards might be seen as a forum to play out those interests.[4]

Their responsibility for financial oversight requires that boards have sufficient financial acumen to assess, question, and advise on the multi-million-dollar, often multi-billion-dollar operating and capital budgets of their universities. Some members with professional accounting designations must staff their audit and finance committees. They know how to read and understand financial statements (some board members can do neither) and must do extensive preparation for meetings. They must bring their experience to the board table and ask the right questions about the university's financial viability, investments, pensions, and other commitments.

Responsibility for financial oversight carries with it board engagement in strategic planning. The budget cannot be approved without understanding and approving the context in which it is proposed, including the university's goals and direction, and means of achieving them.

Because universities are often engaged in large capital projects, it is helpful if their board numbers include people with significant levels of experience with the construction industry. Boards must approve financial contracts and spending commitments for new buildings, renovations, deferred maintenance, information technology, and other major equipment purchases, and they must be diligent in determining that the university's managers have done what they needed to do to ensure that the terms, including prices, are reasonable.

Experience with government is another important attribute that should be found among board members. Governments remain the single most important partner of Canadian public universities. They are their largest funder and they are associated by the public with university shortcomings and successes. Governments pay attention to universities, though with varying degrees of comprehension. Some post-secondary ministers bring discernment and wisdom to their relationships with universities; others lack these qualities yet seek to force their hand in discussions with them. All post-secondary ministers, together with their colleagues in government, including the occupant of the premier's chair, must be known to university leaders, and must be engaged by them in conversations that foster mutual understanding, goodwill, and hopefully, sound public policy.

Board members who have had experience in or with government, and who know the government actors, can better advise, warn, encourage, and support their university administrations in their relationships with them. With the assent of the board chair and president, they may be able to add their voices to the conversations that take place.

Considering the breadth and depth of university board responsibilities, we might expect to see high priority placed on populating boards with people who have the relevant qualifications and experience. But this is not the case. In the Carleton example two members are ex officio; twelve originate from within the university and are elected or appointed by university bodies or interests. Backgrounds and experience relevant to the board duties described above are not what brings these members onto the board; if they have relevant experience, it is only by happenstance. The remaining eighteen, as we have seen, are the public members of the board. In the Canadian experience generally, public members are not appointed to university boards only because their backgrounds commend them for this kind of service; they are often present because they are favoured by the appointing government authority for extraneous reasons. Carleton is fortunate in this respect because the board picks all of its public members through a nominating committee. This facilitates the best practice of appointing them according to a skills matrix matching positions to board personnel needs, and to candidates with the requisite backgrounds to lead and staff major board committees: executive, governance, audit, finance, property, capital planning, and others. These public members are at arm's length from particular university interests, and a review of their backgrounds reveals that Carleton has been fortunate in attracting highly qualified people.

But the Carleton Board, at thirty-two members, is too large. Historically, Canadian university boards have ranged in size from eleven to more than sixty members, but experience has shown the optimum number to be much closer to the bottom end of this spectrum than to the top: eighteen members may be about right. This number enables the board to function more as a committee of the whole as distinct from a model in which a small executive committee leads a much larger board. But the constituency factor makes this number impossible at most Canadian universities, including Carleton. With two ex officio members and twelve others elected or appointed by internal bodies, the number of members must exceed twenty-eight for public members to be in the majority.

The constituency factor is felt in other ways. Sometimes faculty, staff, and students are as conscious (or more so) of the interests of those who put them on the board as they are of their duty as governors to address the issues before them in the best interests of the university. Though never explicit, they may sometimes equate particular insider interests and those of the university. Students are in a particularly difficult situation here because of the perennially hot button tuition issue, but faculty and staff, too, have interests because of their employment. In part, these interests can be addressed through the classic distinction between being a delegate of an appointing or electing body, and serving as its representative.[5] It is naive, however, to believe that this distinction fully resolves the issues. Conflicts of interest are present at the board table, perhaps obvious, perhaps subtle. They are sometimes, though not always, articulated, and often not fully addressed.

Two further considerations are notable. The first is time. Internal members are on the board by virtue of office, or as a result of election or nomination of a university body. Those employed by the university are still being paid when attending board meetings. As we have seen, this is not so for public members. They are unpaid volunteers who are taking time away from their normal commitments to serve the university. They are, typically, busy people, many of them in professional offices or practices from which their absence for board commitments represents a financial sacrifice as well as a contribution to public service. Their enthusiasm for this service is naturally affected by conditions on the board. Efficient meetings, focused on the important work to be done, in the company of board colleagues who share their commitment and focus make the experience worthwhile. Efficient, effective boards usually have an esprit de corps that brings its members together in common cause. They may not agree, but their disagreements are civil. Unduly protracted meetings in which they are deflected from board business by fractious behaviour of one or more board members make the experience more of a burden, which may lead to frustration, departure, refusals of second terms, or even discouragement from accepting appointments in the first place. How the board and its members conduct their business matters.

And so we come to codes of conduct. In January 2016 Carleton's Board of Governors approved a code of conduct. There is no doubt about its legal authority to do so; boards have important work to do and have latitude in determining how they will conduct their business by enacting bylaws and other rules. And with the variety of members with different backgrounds and representing different interests, clarity about roles and responsibilities is necessary for university boards to come together productively, and to do the work assigned to them by legislation or charter. This is not to say that a code of conduct is essential for all of them. Bylaws may suffice for some; others may have a well-developed consensus and culture around board governance that is accepted by all. In others, historical differences and current tensions may be such that a code of conduct is necessary to establish what the board as a whole expects of individual board members. It is not wildly speculative to suggest that the adoption of a board code of conduct at Carleton originated with or was hastened by Gorelick's membership.

We now have the context for the present case. Early in his appointment as a new board member, Gorelick posted that his focus in reporting on the board's public meetings "is and will be on due process" but that he would also "discuss substantive matters, especially as related to [his] constituency."[6] In a later blog he observed that a board colleague had taken a position that "makes his lack of due process and naked rejection of the rule of law … appalling."[7] He also accused the board of using "a totalitarian strong-arm tactic,"[8] and the board and executive of taking a "totalitarian and Orwellian approach."[9] He described the university administration as "urinating away monies,"[10] and the board chair's ruling on one of his many points of order as "brazen and shameless."[11] He opined, too, that "the full board of governors at Carleton University are more akin to parliament with duly elected members, than its cabinet."[12] And he offered his opinion on a collective disadvantage of the eighteen public board members: "There exists a term-of-art for those who represent the entire universe of stakeholders, namely, at large. Carleton University should be familiar with that terminology insofar as its Board of Governors has eighteen 'at-large' members chosen from 'the community,' which apparently means anybody except current faculty and students ... These eighteen at-large members do not necessarily view community interests through academic eyes and therefore do not necessarily understand the importance of academic freedom."[13]

His denunciation of the board of which he was a member continued. The president's and board executive's understanding of the difference between open and closed meetings was in a "perverted state."[14] Carleton's governance was "hierarchical, authoritarian and corporate."[15] There is "rampant corporatization"[16] of Carleton's board. And "it is no wonder that most of the Carleton University community has lost confidence in its board of governors."[17]

It is not possible to capture here the full impact of these attacks by Gorelick on his board colleagues. Reading them in the context of the entire blog leads to the conclusion that the board was deflected from its normal agendas to deal with the attacks and their fallout, including the protracted procedural debates to which they led. This deflection did not last for a week or two, but for more than a year. That is a serious problem in itself, given the importance to the university, and to the public, of the effective and efficient discharge of board duties. It is a problem, too, in the challenge of attracting and retaining qualified people to undertake public service of this kind. But the problems only begin there. Attacks of this kind are felt by other board members and have a deleterious effect on board meetings. Trust and civility are important to boards, and they can be undermined by the conduct of only one of their members.

And Gorelick was one of their members – not an observer from the sidelines. His attacks on his fellow board members could only have been fuelled by the misunderstanding of his role that is evident in his blog. His reference to his constituents; his orientation to due process rather than to the due diligence that is required of boards; and his comparison of the board to a parliament with elected members, and presumably an official opposition of which he was the leader or a member, all suggest that he did not understand board governance. His disparagement of the eighteen public board members follows from this concept of the board: they are members "at large" who don't have a constituency and do not necessarily share the constituency representatives' views of community interests and academic freedom. They are, in other words, second-class board members.

Serious as they are, these issues could more easily be set aside if they were the idiosyncratic views of one person who has since left the Carleton board because he would not conform to expected member conduct. But Gorelick's faculty union and the Canadian Association of University Teachers have rallied to his side. So division in the commons widens, and we must ask why. To answer we must turn to the accusation of CAUT: Carleton University is suppressing Gorelick's academic freedom and free speech rights.

The case we explored in chapter 1 and the present case illustrate what is widely known in the Canadian university world: there is no consensus on the definition and ambit of academic freedom. We have noted differences between the approaches to the issue by Universities Canada and CAUT, and we turn now to those differences to explore their meaning and significance.

We must first acknowledge the common ground here. All people within universities, or who understand them, appreciate that academic freedom is a necessary condition for their activities. Scholars must be free to explore whatever topics they deem appropriate, in whatever ways they judge necessary, in both their teaching and research, and to disseminate their views thereon without constraint. Academic freedom is essential to the integrity and quality of university work; without it the university mission fails. We must acknowledge, too, that robust free speech must be present alongside academic freedom in the university commons. The latter, it will be argued here, has more limited scope than is often attributed to it, but academic freedom is not the only protection of speech. What is not safeguarded by academic freedom may be covered by freedom of expression.

We should recognize that neither academic freedom nor freedom of speech can be taken for granted. We saw in chapter 3 that freedom of expression is threatened with demotion in our commons, from paramount value to one among others. And history teaches us that academic freedom requires regular affirmation and vigilance in its protection. It also requires clarity in definition so that threats can be accurately identified and repelled, and that all within and beyond our universities understand its centrality to their mission.

Within a month in 2011, both Universities Canada and the Canadian Association of University Teachers released updated policies on academic freedom. The UC statement[18] provides:

> Academic freedom is the freedom to teach and conduct research in an academic environment. Academic freedom is fundamental to the mandate of universities to pursue truth, educate students and disseminate knowledge and understanding.
>
> In teaching, academic freedom is fundamental to the protection of the rights of the teacher to teach and of the student to learn. In research and scholarship, it is critical to advancing knowledge.
>
> Academic freedom includes the right to freely communicate knowledge and the results of research and scholarship.
>
> Unlike the broader concept of freedom of speech, academic freedom must be based on institutional integrity, rigorous standards for enquiry and institutional standards for autonomy, which allows universities to set their research and educational priorities.

The Universities Canada statement stipulates that academic freedom exists for important social purposes: "Academic freedom is essential to the role of universities in a democratic society. Universities are committed to the pursuit of truth and its communication to others, including students and the broader community. To do this faculty must be free to take intellectual risks and tackle controversial subjects in their teaching, research and scholarship." And on the limits of academic freedom, the statement continues:

> Academic freedom is constrained by the professional standards of the relevant discipline and the responsibility of the institution to organize its academic mission. The insistence on professional standards speaks to the rigor of the enquiry and not to its outcome.

The constraint of institutional requirements recognizes simply that the academic mission, like other work, has to be organized according to institutional needs. This includes the institution's needs to select and appoint faculty and staff, to admit and discipline students, to establish and control curriculum, to make organizational arrangements for the conduct of academic work, to certify completion of a program and to grant degrees.

The statement further imposes responsibilities on university leaders to protect and promote academic freedom, to lead in communicating the values around academic freedom, and to defend the concept against claims that are excessive or too loose. Faculty members and university leaders both "have an obligation to ensure that students' human rights are respected and that they are encouraged to pursue their education according to the principles of academic freedom."[19]

The Canadian Association of University Teachers statement[20] provides:

Academic freedom includes the right, without restriction by prescribed doctrine, to freedom to teach and discuss; freedom to carry out research and to disseminate the results thereof; freedom to produce and perform creative works; freedom to engage in service to the institution and the community; freedom to express one's opinion about the institution, its administration, and the system in which one works; freedom to acquire, preserve and provide access to documentary material in all formats; and freedom to participate in professional and representative academic bodies. Academic freedom always entails freedom from institutional censorship ...

All academic staff must have the right to fulfill their functions without reprisal or repression by the institution, the state, or any other source ...

All academic staff have the right to freedom of thought, conscience, religion, expression, assembly and association, and the right to liberty and security of the person and freedom of movement. Academic staff must not be hindered or impeded in exercising their civil rights as individuals including the right to contribute to social change through free expression of opinion on matters of public interest. Academic staff must not suffer any institutional penalties because of the exercise of such rights.

The statements are set out here to compare them and identify the divide between them; it is a substantial divide with important implications. The first difference between the two is that the UC statement purports to be complete on the subject of academic freedom; the CAUT statement does not. This difference is evident in the opening words of each statement ("academic freedom *is* ..." and "academic freedom *includes* ..."). CAUT implies there is something more to the subject than what is detailed in its statement. This difference invites the question "what more is there?" and the CAUT statement leaves the question unanswered. This contributes to the lack of clarity in identifying the parameters of academic freedom.

The second difference is that the UC statement grounds academic freedom in teaching and research, and in the dissemination of the latter; the CAUT statement does not. This difference takes us into the history of academic freedom and its developing rationale. "It was ... in nineteenth-century Germany that the modern conception of academic freedom came to be formulated. The idea of the university as a place where scholars are to pursue truth, as well as to formulate it and transfer it to students, who at the same time come to pursue truth for themselves, came to be dominant there ... Intellectual discipline over the members of the university community is excluded, lest it distort their search."[21]

The University of Berlin's Friedrich Paul Paulsen expanded on this in writing, "It is no longer, as formerly, the function of a university teacher to hand down a body of truth as established by authorities, but to search after scientific knowledge by investigation, and to teach his hearers to do the same ... For the academic teacher and his hearers there can be no prescribed and no proscribed thoughts. There is only one rule for instruction: to justify the truth of one's teaching by reason and the facts."[22]

It is clear that these origins grounded academic freedom in teaching and research. It is equally clear that, since these origins, there has evolved recognition that protection from institutional censorship or discipline extended beyond the classroom, study, and laboratory.[23] Academics are citizens, too, and they participate as such in their service and voluntary capacities. They must be free to do so. The landmark 1940 (updated in 1970) Statement of Principles of Academic Freedom and Tenure in the United States[24] provides:

> 1. Teachers are entitled to full freedom in research and in the publication of results, subject to the adequate performance of their other academic duties; but research for pecuniary return should be based upon an understanding with the authorities of the institution.
>
> 2. Teachers are entitled to freedom in the classroom in discussing their subject, but they should be careful not to introduce into their teaching controversial matter that has no relation to their subject. Limitations of academic freedom because of religious or other aims of the institution should be clearly stated in writing at the time of the appointment.
>
> 3. College and university professors are citizens, members of a learned profession, and officers of an educational institution. When they speak or write as citizens, they should be free from institutional censorship or discipline, but their special position in the community imposes special obligations. As scholars and educational officers, they should remember that the public may judge their profession and their institution by their utterances. Hence they should at all times be accurate; should exercise appropriate restraint; should show respect for the opinions of others, and should make every effort to indicate that they are not speaking for the institution.

This is a compelling statement for a number of reasons. It was endorsed both by what is now the Association of American Colleges and Universities, and by the American Association of University Professors.[25] Compare this with the situation in Canada, in which there are two different statements offered by UC and CAUT and little potential for their reconciliation in the interests of a common university voice on a subject as important as academic freedom.

The content of the American statement is compelling too. "Full freedom" in research and publication combined with "freedom" in the classroom are reminders of the German origins of modern academic freedom. With respect to the latter, there is a caution about sticking to the subject matter of the course, and a limitation pertaining to faith-based institutions, but in general, the first two paragraphs of the statement would attract wide if not universal concurrence.

So would the third paragraph. It recognizes that academic status confers upon its holders opportunities and even duties (the service and volunteer portfolios of the professoriate) to share their expertise with the public beyond their universities. It encourages them to contribute to the understanding of their fellow citizens, to enlighten and sometimes perhaps to uplift them. Again there are limits, these ones pertaining to their speaking for themselves and not for their universities; and for the importance of respect (for their profession and for others) and accuracy. But, again, there would be no dissent on the merits of the third paragraph.

Apart from the credibility it has by virtue of being a joint statement of professors and university leaders, the American statement provokes two responses bearing on the parameters of academic freedom: first, in addition to differences between the CAUT and UC statements there are important differences between the American and CAUT statements; and second, paragraph 3 in the American statement brings us to the intersection of academic freedom and free speech.

The most striking difference between the two statements is that the American statement acknowledges obligations and responsibilities while the CAUT statement does not. In the latter the word *freedom* is found eleven times; *right* or *rights* are mentioned seven times. Reference to obligations or duties is not to be found. Nor are there any of the cautions or advisories found in the American statement about research for pecuniary return, controversial matter that has no relation to course content, or special obligations when professors speak as citizens. To CAUT, these omissions make for a strong and unqualified statement on academic freedom; to others, the absence of any reference to responsibilities, professional standards, or institutional needs, makes for a statement that is more doctrinal than authoritative. For these reasons, it would not be possible for the CAUT statement to be endorsed by Canadian university leaders in the same way that the American statement has been endorsed by their U.S. counterparts.

The absence of any reference to students, or to an acknowledgment that the obligation to defend academic freedom includes defending the concept against claims in its name that are excessive or too loose, are other reasons why the CAUT statement could not be supported by Canadian university leaders. The latter is a concern in part because the CAUT statement is open-ended on definition. The former is an issue because the question fairly arises: what about the academic freedom of students? There is wide agreement that it is not the same for students as for professors, but student rights in this context are a corollary to faculty rights and merit reference in a statement of this kind.

The third paragraph of the American statement is an acknowledgment that professors are citizens and as such have free speech, though with cautions about its exercise flowing from their status. We could substitute any learned professionals for *college and university professors* and the statement would hold true for them as well. It is therefore accurate for us to summarize the American statement as one that combines academic freedom that respects its modern German origins in paragraphs 1 and 2, with freedom of speech flowing from the First Amendment to the United States Constitution[26] in paragraph 3.

We saw in chapter 3 that freedom of expression is an indispensable condition of the university commons. It complements academic freedom and provides further assurance that voices will not be silenced on account of prevailing orthodoxies, threats, or fears of reprisals, political correctness, or other pressures. It is important in any academic context to distinguish between academic freedom and freedom of expression because, although the latter is a broader concept, its broadest ambit is on the street where any opinion can be held and almost all can be expressed, the only limitation being the law. Off the street there may be limits on freedom of expression because of context, particularly one pertaining to employment.

With this background we can now complete our analysis of the case of Professor Gorelick. Because Carleton University was condemned by CAUT for violating both his academic freedom and free speech rights, we must consider the case on both counts. Because collective agreements in Canada usually address academic freedom, we begin with that document at Carleton.[27] Article 4 provides:

> 4.1 The common good of society depends upon the search for truth and its free exposition. Universities with academic freedom are essential for these purposes both in teaching and scholarship/research. Employees are entitled therefore, to:
>
> (a) freedom in carrying out research and in publishing the results thereof,
> (b) freedom in carrying out teaching and in discussing their subject,
> (c) freedom from institutional censorship.
>
> Academic freedom carries with it the duty to use that freedom in a manner consistent with the scholarly obligation to base research and teaching on an honest search for truth.

The provision, in general, is an unobjectionable statement of academic freedom; the only question is with respect to (c) – freedom from institutional censorship. Underlying CAUT's denunciation and threatened censure may be the argument that requiring Gorelick to adhere to a board code of conduct violates his freedom from institutional censorship. The contrary argument is that this freedom must be understood within the context of Article 4 as a whole, meaning that his freedom from institutional censorship is with respect to his research and teaching, and that requiring Gorelick to adhere to board expectations of member conduct has nothing to do with his research and teaching. The latter is the more compelling argument; there is no absolute freedom here.

But the CAUT and Carleton faculty union argument will not rest on Article 4 alone. They will point to the CAUT statement on the subject and, in particular, the "freedom to express one's opinion about the institution, its administration, and the system in which one works." The argument would be that in authoring his public blog, Gorelick was reporting to his constituents and others, and that the CAUT statement allows him to report in any way he chooses, with whatever comments he wants to make about the board and its members.

Apart from the CAUT statement, there is ample support in Canada for the proposition that academic freedom includes the freedom to criticize one's university, its administration and governance. In the reasons for her opinion in the Berdahl case, the Honourable Lynn Smith stated that commentary on governance falls within the ambit of academic freedom.[28] She further stated, "This does not mean that faculty members who participate in governance, either in representative capacities or as part of the senior administration, might not have additional responsibilities and obligations as a result of those other roles. Those role-specific responsibilities and obligations might serve to limit their freedom to comment on university affairs."[29]

In other words, one who has academic freedom as a faculty member may act in another capacity in which that same freedom is not available. Senior officers of the university are excellent examples. Most of them have academic appointments as well as administrative offices; they retain their academic freedom for any continuing academic work they undertake, but academic freedom is not available to them with respect to their performance of administrative duties. A president cannot claim that her academic freedom protects her from the consequences of her administrative decisions or justifies negative comments she might make about governing bodies. So, too, Gorelick had academic freedom with respect to his continuing academic responsibilities but he did not have it with respect to his board membership. His obligations as a board member were to the board and its work, and his academic freedom as a faculty member cannot explain or justify his behaviour in that capacity.

The free speech argument fails for the same reason. Gorelick is entitled to express his views on the board and board members on the street, in the university commons, or on his blog now that he is no longer a board member.[30] But as a board member his free speech was contained by board rules and protocols about how the board goes about its business, and what the board in general expects of its members.

We may now conclude. This account commands our attention not because of what Gorelick did or did not do, but because of the endorsement of his actions by his union and CAUT. This suggests a wider sense of academic freedom that is at odds with its origins and continuing rationale. Perhaps the explanation lies in the CAUT statement with its open-ended extrapolation on academic freedom and which, in comparison to both the UC and American statements, is long on freedoms and rights, and short on responsibilities.

The narrative also commands our attention because it reveals shortcomings in understanding university governance that defy explanation. Boards of governors have much important work to do on behalf of the public and the university, and must determine how the work is to be done collectively and by individual members. It should be obvious to any careful observer that Gorelick's conduct was at odds with precepts of sound board governance, and that his continued membership on the board was untenable. But it was not obvious to his union and CAUT, and that may be the most troubling feature in the story of Carleton's board blogger.

Freedom of Religion in the Commons: A Law School for Trinity Western University?

Trinity Western is an evangelical Christian university whose mission is to develop "godly Christian leaders: positive, goal-oriented university graduates with thoroughly Christian minds, growing disciples of Jesus Christ who glorify God by fulfilling the Great Commission, serving God and people in the various marketplaces of life."[1] It is a private university that does not receive operating or capital funds from government. Its core values are closely aligned with its mission, and its students are required to sign a community covenant that contains a pledge to abstain from sexual intimacy outside of marriage between one man and one woman.

Trinity Western seeks to add legal education to its program offerings. In 2012 it submitted its law school proposal to the Federation of Law Societies of Canada and to the British Columbia Ministry of Advanced Education. The former's approval rested upon the proposal meeting the national competency requirement endorsed by all provincial law societies, and in late 2013 the federation's Common Law Degree Approval Committee concluded that it did so. It was "comprehensive and ... designed to ensure that students acquired each competency" required.[2] Soon afterwards, British Columbia Cabinet member Amrik Virk stated, "As Advanced Education Minister, I have granted consent for Trinity Western University's application for its proposed new law school program."[3]

The seemingly clear path ahead proved anything but. On 11 April 2014 the British Columbia Law Society's benchers (governors) voted 20–6 in favour of accrediting the new school, but opposition was coalescing in British Columbia and elsewhere.[4] Law firms in Toronto and Vancouver launched a lawsuit aimed at reversing Minister Virk's decision giving TWU the go-ahead on the law school.[5] In June, more than three thousand of BC's thirteen thousand lawyers voted on a non-binding resolution to reverse the accreditation decision, and the Law Society responded by directing a further vote on a resolution declaring that "the proposed law school at Trinity Western University is not an approved faculty of law for the purposes of the Law Society's admission program."[6] This time eight thousand of the society's members voted, 74 per cent of them in support of the motion, and the benchers reversed their earlier decision in favour of accreditation. Weeks later, Minister Virk announced, "Based on the current situation, I have decided to revoke my approval of the proposed law school at Trinity Western University. This means the university cannot enroll any students in its proposed program."[7]

Results were mixed in other provinces and territories. Alberta, Saskatchewan, Prince Edward Island, Newfoundland and Labrador, and Nunavut adopted the federation's decision approving the program. Manitoba's benchers decided to monitor processes and decisions in other jurisdictions in support of approaching the issue on a national basis. Ontario's benchers voted 28–21 to reject Trinity Western's application for accreditation. Nova Scotia made accreditation conditional upon the university withdrawing its covenant or exempting law students from it. The Council of the Law Society of New Brunswick affirmed by a close margin its earlier decision to accredit the program notwithstanding a non-binding vote of members against doing so.

Results were mixed in the courts as well. In December 2014 TWU indicated that it would challenge the positions taken by BC, Ontario, and Nova Scotia on its proposed law school.[8] British Columbia and Nova Scotia courts ruled in favour of the TWU challenge, Ontario courts against. In British Columbia, the chief justice of the province's Supreme Court concluded: "I find that the Benchers improperly fettered their discretion and acted outside their authority in delegating to the [Law Society of British

Columbia's] members the question of whether TWU's proposed faculty of law should be approved for the purposes of the admissions program. Even if I am wrong, and the Benchers had the authority to delegate the decision to its members, I find that the decision was made without proper consideration of the Charter rights at issue, and therefore cannot stand."[9]

The appropriate remedy, ruled the chief justice, was to invalidate the decision based on the referendum outcome, and to restore the results of the 11 April/14 vote of the benchers approving the TWU program.[10]

The Law Society appealed this decision to the British Columbia Court of Appeal. The case was heard over three days in June 2016 by a panel of five appellate justices, and their unanimous decision dismissing the appeal was released in November 2016.[11] In the Court's view, the question before them was whether the Law Society's decision not to approve TWU's proposed law school was reasonable. "Answering that question requires us to consider conflicting and strongly-held views, and to reconcile competing rights. On one side are the rights, freedoms and aspirations of lesbian, gay, bisexual, transgendered and queer (LGBTQ) persons and their place in a progressive and tolerant society; on the other are the religious freedom and rights of association of evangelical Christians who sincerely hold the beliefs described in the Covenant and nurtured by TWU."[12] The Court acknowledged that TWU's covenant treated LGBTQ persons unequally. "We note that it is the Covenant's definition of marriage 'between a man and a woman' that is at issue in these proceedings. The Covenant prohibits all expressions of sexual intimacy outside of marriage, regardless of sexual orientation; in that respect all students are treated equally. However, the Covenant recognizes the marriage of heterosexual couples only; expressions of sexual intimacy between same-sex married couples remains prohibited. It is in this respect that LGBTQ persons are treated unequally."[13]

The Court recognized four issues raised by the appeal:

1. Did the Law Society have statutory authority to refuse to approve TWU's law school on the basis of an admissions policy?

2. Did the benchers unlawfully sub-delegate or fetter their decision-making authority?
3. Was TWU denied procedural fairness?
4. Does the Law Society's decision reasonably balance the statutory objectives of the Legal Profession Act against the religious freedom rights of TWU?

In summary, the Court answered the questions: 1 – yes; 2 – yes; 3 – no; 4 – no. The fourth question and answer are of particular interest here. The Court of Appeal stated:

> The TWU community has a right to hold, and act on its beliefs, absence evidence of actual harm. To do so is an expression of its right to freedom of religion. The Law Society's decision not to approve TWU's faculty of law denies these evangelical Christians the ability to fundamental religious and associative rights which would otherwise be assured to them under s.2 of the Charter.
>
> In light of the severe impact of non-approval on the religious freedom rights at stake and the minimal impact of approval on the access of LGBTQ persons to law school and the legal profession ... we conclude that a decision to declare TWU not to be an approved law faculty would be unreasonable.[14]

In Nova Scotia, a Supreme Court trial judge concluded that the Nova Scotia Barristers' Society did not have the authority to make accreditation of the TWU program conditional upon the university withdrawing its covenant or exempting law students from it. Even if it did have that authority, "it did not exercise it in a way that reasonably considered the concerns for religious freedom and liberty of conscience."[15] The Barristers' Society was unsuccessful in its appeal to the Nova Scotia Court of Appeal[16] and decided not to appeal to the Supreme Court of Canada.

In Ontario, TWU applied to the Divisional Court for judicial review of the decision of the Ontario Law Society not to accredit its proposed law program. The application was dismissed and the university appealed to the Ontario Court of Appeal. The appeal was heard in early June 2016 by three appellate justices, and their unanimous judgment was delivered later in the same month. Writing for the Court, Justice MacPherson found that the Ontario Law Society's decision "fell squarely within its statutory mandate to act in the public interest,"[17] and that the appropriate standard for review was reasonableness.[18] Was the decision not to accredit TWU's law school reasonable? "In assessing the reasonableness of the [Ontario Law Society's] decision, this court must consider it in the context of (i) the appellant's Charter rights at stake; (ii) the [Law Society's] statutory objectives; and (iii) whether the decision represents a reasonable balance between the two."[19]

Adopting a broad definition of freedom of religion, the Court concluded that there were Charter rights at stake and found that the Ontario Law Society's decision infringed TWU's Charter right of religious freedom.[20] The Court also found that the infringement occurred in pursuit of the Law Society's statutory objectives: the Law Society "has been engaged in determining the requirements of a legal education, necessary for the purposes of qualifying individuals for admission to the Bar, for more than 200 years."[21]

> In carrying out its mandate under its enabling statute, the (Law Society) throughout its long history, has acted to remove obstacles based on considerations, other than ones based on merit, such as religious affiliation, race and gender, so as to provide previously excluded groups the opportunity to obtain a legal education and thus become members of the legal profession in Ontario.
>
> In keeping with that tradition, throughout those many years, the [Law Society] has acted to remove all barriers to entry to the legal profession save one – merit.[22]

The remaining issue is whether the Law Society's decision not to accredit TWU's proposed law school reflected a reasonable balance between TWU's Charter right to freedom of religion, and the Law Society's pursuit of its statutory objectives. The Court of Appeal found that it did: "Taking account of the extent of the impact on TWU's freedom of religion and the [Law Society's] mandate to act in the public interest, the decision to not accredit TWU represents a reasonable balance between TWU's 2(a) right under the Charter and the [Law Society's] statutory objectives."[23]

The conflicting decisions of the British Columbia and Ontario Courts of Appeal set the stage for the Supreme Court of Canada decision to come. It will not be the first time that TWU went to Canada's highest court to advance its views on the scope of religious freedom. In an earlier case[24] the university resisted a decision by the British Columbia College of Teachers denying its application for full responsibility for a teacher education program. Because the university's community standards included denunciation of homosexuality as a sexual sin that was biblically condemned, the college determined that it would be contrary to the public interest to give its approval. The college's jurisdiction to so decide was at issue and so was its finding of discrimination here. On application for judicial review, the BC Supreme Court found against the College of Teachers on both counts: it did not have jurisdiction under the Teaching Profession Act to consider whether the TWU program followed discriminatory practices, and there was no reasonable foundation for a finding of discrimination. The British Columbia Court of Appeal disagreed with the trial judge on jurisdiction but affirmed his decision on the basis that discrimination could not be established. The Supreme Court of Canada dismissed the appeal from this decision. "The proper place to draw the line in cases like the one at bar is generally between belief and conduct. Absent concrete evidence that training teachers at TWU fosters discrimination in the public schools of B.C., the freedom of individuals to adhere to certain religious beliefs while at TWU should be respected ... For better or for worse, tolerance of divergent beliefs is a hallmark of a democratic society."[25]

We return, then, to a theme prominent in chapter 3 and found elsewhere in this book: tolerance. Emphasizing this theme, there is a lot of room in our university commons, room for Trinity Western University and room for the eight other approved teacher education programs in British Columbia. Provided there is no discrimination in fact, we are in the realm of religious belief engaging Charter protection that is not outweighed by other rights and values.

In general, the case law reveals a broad scope for freedom of religion, leaving difficult issues to be resolved within the context of balancing rights in apparent conflict, in the above cases between religious freedom and equality rights. By proceeding in this way, important questions are left unaddressed. Are all beliefs held in common by adherents of a particular religion, denomination, or sect, religious beliefs to be afforded constitutional protection? Are all policies and actions pursuant to these common beliefs to be seen as expressions of freedom of religion invoking constitutional protection? If they are, the approach in the case law is appropriate, indeed inevitable. If they are not, we must confront more directly the meaning of freedom of religion in a modern, pluralistic society so that we can determine when it is properly invoked.

In Canada we have no difficulty in the exclusive realms of conscience and belief. Individuals are free to believe what they want or choose to believe, whether as a result of reflection, teaching, tradition, indoctrination, or other influence. Nor do we have difficulty in recognizing that religious observance is typically a communal activity bringing together fellow worshipers for their devotional activities. They must organize their worshipful activities, and so we recognize their freedom to secure places for them, to determine requirements for church membership, and for participation in their observances. This is, we would say, their own business. We become hesitant only when they move beyond their worshipful activities and into a public domain shared with others who do not believe and worship as they do. We might think it unlikely that a religious community would open a medical clinic, grocery store, or a cinema, though it would be free to do so. We would expect, though, that in embarking on these activities it would adhere to standards that are not their own for offering medical services, selling groceries, or showing movies. Provincial human rights law is instructive in this respect. When offering services to the public, religious groups should not be at liberty to impose discriminatory faith-based requirements in delivering those services.

Education may be private, or it may be offered to the public. When it is the latter the sponsoring agency – in Canada – is usually though not always public. Trinity Western University is a private institution, but it proclaims that its doors are open to all who are academically qualified to enter them. In offering services to the public, the university's claim to religious freedom in imposing a faith-based requirement (the covenant) is assailable on the basis that it is not the agency that counts; what matters is that discrimination in offering services to the public is impermissible in Canada.

We might anticipate Trinity Western University to answer this argument by renewing its claim that the covenant is non-discriminatory and, if this claim fails, to persist in its view that as a private institution it is free to require its students to sign. If all of its students were from its faith base, this answer might prevail. But TWU recruits students from beyond that base, whether for a sustainable head count, or for proselytizing and other reasons. When the university offers its services to the public at large, it enters the domain in which discrimination on prohibited grounds is or should be impermissible.

Any claim that the covenant is non-discriminatory should fail. Both the Ontario Court of Appeal and its counterpart in British Columbia acknowledged that it treated LGBTQ persons unequally, and a compelling argument to the contrary is not in sight. And so we come to the public-private distinction. Here the argument is that TWU receives no operating or capital funding from government and accordingly has greater latitude in conducting its affairs than public institutions. We can begin here by making an uncontroversial observation. It would not be open to any public university to require adherence to a covenant identical to the one in place at TWU. Why any public institution would want to do so is a good question, of course, but setting it aside for the purposes of argument, the covenant would be out of the question for public institutions, even if for some reason it appealed to them. Now that we have established that TWU has entered the public domain to offer educational services to the public, the only non-academic distinction between it and other universities is that it is the educational arm of a religious community. Does this feature leave it free to treat LGBTQ applicants differently from others?

The answer should be no for two reasons. The first we just considered: whether public or private TWU is offering its services to the public and it is in this dimension that normal human rights protection is invoked. Second, the public/private distinction is not as compelling as first it might appear. Although the university declares that it receives no public operating or capital funding, its intersections with the public domain are many. It is incorporated by an act of the British Columbia Legislature and it receives public dollars and the very considerable public benefits from being designated a charity by the Canada Revenue Agency. It was awarded $2.6 million from the federal government's Knowledge Infrastructure Plan. It has four Canada Research Chairs funded by the Government of Canada. Its faculty are eligible for tri-council and other public research funding. Tuition tax credits and the Canada student loan program benefit TWU students as they do those at public institutions. In reality, Canadian taxpayers provide considerable and ongoing support for the activities of Trinity Western University. It is not unique in this respect. Catholic schools collect school taxes in support of differences from their public school counterparts that are driven by religion freedom, and other faith-based institutions derive some of the same benefits from public dollars as are gained by TWU. The support of public dollars is not determinative, but it does weaken the claim that TWU is free to depart from Canadian public policy because it is a private institution.

The burden of this argument is not that Trinity Western's freedom of religion as expressed by its covenant may have to yield to others' Charter or human rights; it is that freedom of religion is not engaged in these circumstances and should not be available to the university in defence of its covenant. In offering its services to the public, for which it receives considerable public support, TWU has moved beyond the realm of religious doctrine and worshipful activities in which its freedom of religion is uncontroversial. It has claimed and established a place in the domain of offering educational services to the public and, in this domain, its religious tenets are immaterial. Non-discrimination in offering these services to the public is what matters here.

Even if this view of the case does not prevail, it must at least carry weight in the balancing of rights approach that we have seen thus far in the courts. In particular, let us revisit an important paragraph in the judgment of the British Columbia Court of Appeal: "In light of the severe impact of non-approval (of the TWU law school) on the religious freedom rights at stake and the minimal impact of approval on the access of LGBTQ persons to law school and the legal profession ... we conclude that a decision to declare TWU not to be an approved law faculty would be unreasonable."[26]

In other words, LGBTQ persons can go to law school elsewhere. This is reminiscent of answers to allegations of discrimination that we have seen throughout the ages. It would be unfortunate if it prevailed in this context.

The Trinity Western law school story raises a broader subject: the recognition of faith-based institutions in Canada. Religious affiliation per se is not their distinguishing feature; many Canadian universities were founded by churches and some have continuing connections to religious orders.[27] Faith-based institutions have a tighter relationship as indicated in this definition: "A faith test in the fullest sense requires that a candidate for appointment or continuing employment in a university will affirm he or she is a practicing Christian. The affirming person will then say that his or her private and public life will be ordered according to Christian doctrine and under policies agreed by the administration and Board."[28] "The test does not stop with religious conviction. It goes on to require ... that an academic or other employee will not criticize the university or its policy in public or in the academic community."[29]

Faith tests falling within this or similar definitions provoke additional questions about the place of religious belief and practice in the university commons. Among them is whether degree-granting institutions with these tests are eligible for membership in Universities Canada. Membership is important to them. For constitutional and historical reasons, there is no formal accreditation system for our degree-granting institutions, and membership in Universities Canada is widely seen, within Canada and abroad, as an imprimatur of academic respectability. The organization is also well known and respected by governments and the public as the most important national voice of our universities and colleges, and these institutions understand the importance of being part of that voice. Further, Universities Canada, through its meetings, resources, and outreach, provides opportunities, support, and credibility for individual and collective member access to the corridors of power that affect their activities.

In autumn 2016 the institutional members of Universities Canada approved a new criterion for membership: "With respect to all institutional policies and practices, the institution affirms its commitment to equal treatment of all persons without discrimination on the basis of race, religious belief, colour, gender, physical or mental disability, age, ancestry, place of origin, marital status, family status, sex, and sexual orientation, or other grounds identified in applicable human rights law."[30]

Universities Canada and its predecessor, the Association of Universities and Colleges of Canada, had struggled with the issue of faith-based institutional membership for years.[31] When Trinity Western first sought membership in 1984, its application was the subject of considerable debate, and a special committee was established to consider how to address future applications from like institutions. The committee proposed an approach similar to that in the United States: membership would be permitted provided the institution made clear its statement of faith and implications for academic freedom.[32] This approach was approved by the AUCC Board, though it is notable that concerns at the time were directed more to academic freedom than they were to discrimination. That changed when in 1991 the King's College (now the King's University) in Edmonton was admitted to membership. Contemporaneously, the case of Delwin Vriend was beginning to unfold.

[Vriend] was employed as a laboratory coordinator by King's College ... He was given a permanent, full-time position in 1988. Throughout his term of employment he received positive evaluations, salary increases and promotions for his work performance. On February 20, 1990, in response to an inquiry by the president of the college, Vriend disclosed that he was homosexual. In early January, 1991, the board of governors of the college adopted a position statement on homosexuality, and shortly thereafter, the president of the college requested Vriend's resignation. He declined to resign ... and Vriend's employment was terminated by the college. The sole reason given for his termination was his non-compliance with the policy of the college on homosexual practice.[33]

It is not surprising that other members of Universities Canada would ask whether they shared affinity with colleagues that would fire a person for this reason. Theirs is a non-governmental, fee-paying membership organization – with wide discretion to determine their own membership criteria – and their raison d'être is a common educational mission, not one clouded by discriminatory behaviour that most of them find repugnant. Although the case was ultimately decided in Vriend's favour by the Supreme Court of Canada,[34] it was a catalyst for a reconsideration of institutional membership criteria that ultimately resulted in the new 2016 membership criterion.[35]

It is unlikely that the issues have been put to rest. New applicants for Universities Canada membership will be required to affirm the new criterion immediately; current members will be obliged to affirm it by 2020. It is possible that some will not do so under the umbrella of freedom of religion, and the organization will face the prospect of ending the membership of one or more of them. The policy has already been greeted by protests[36] and they can be expected to continue as 2020 approaches. More importantly, the new criterion will not bring final clarity to the issue. We can expect it to be tested further, and for difficult questions at the intersection of religion and the university commons to persist.

A Universities Canada policy statement accompanied the announcement of its new membership criterion. "For further legal clarity, and to minimize potential misinterpretation of the criterion," the statement reads, it must be clear that a membership institution

> does not allow discrimination against faculty, staff and students in all aspects of their employment and/or education based on Protected Grounds, including but not limited to hiring faculty and staff, the employment relationship or the termination of the employment relationship, selection and admission of students, and the discipline or

expulsion of students. Having due regard to the fundamental principle of non-discrimination ... the institution will not impose any occupational requirements in an employment relationship that would have the effect of discriminating on Protected Grounds, unless such requirements are bona fide occupational requirements that are permitted under applicable rights law. For further certainty, nothing in this policy prohibits ameliorative programs, specified institutions or programs, academic/professional codes of conduct or the enforcement of such codes of conduct, provided that none of the terms of the code of conduct are related to Protected Grounds.[37]

It is to be remembered that what is at stake here is membership in Universities Canada, not government approval, formal accreditation, or other public recognition. Faith-based institutions that do not seek membership, or that choose to withdraw from the organization, can continue to operate as they have in the past, subject to federal and provincial law. Those that seek to apply or to retain current membership have two choices: to challenge the new criterion and policy, or to conform to its requirements.

The former would rest on establishing that the issue of UC membership is justiciable (determinable by a court) and that the new criterion is unreasonable. Both are substantial hurdles, but if membership in the organization is established as a de facto accreditation requirement, Universities Canada may be subject to public law requirements for its membership decisions. If so, it is likely that the first hurdle is cleared and the path open to further argument on whether the new membership criterion is an unreasonable intrusion of the religious freedom of faith-based institutions. It may be that the Supreme Court of Canada decision in the law school case will assist in resolving that question.

Another important question is whether faith-based institutions are permitted to discriminate in favour of their religious adherents in hiring decisions. The question is open to argument on the language of the criterion, but the Universities Canada policy explicitly acknowledges that "a faith-based institution hiring based on faith can continue to do so."[38] The policy also states that "special programs to promote equity – for example, increasing the number of women faculty, or programs to help indigenize the academic community"[39] – are not precluded by the policy.

A further question arises as to whether a faith-based institution that hires on the basis of faith can fire on the basis of faith. What happens to an employee who experiences a change or loss of faith subsequent to her appointment? What happens if a change or loss of faith leads the employee to teach contrary to its precepts or to publicly question them in debate, scholarship, or speaking engagements? The same argument that allows hiring based on faith would seem to support firing based on faith. The purpose of both is to safeguard the institution's faith orientation and commitment. The Universities Canada policy is silent on this issue and so the answer may lie in the language of the faith test and the employment contract. If it is a condition of employment that the employee be among the university's faith base, a subsequent withdrawal from that faith breaches (or frustrates) the contract and may end the employment relationship. And if being among the university's faith base means living and espousing abstention from sexual intimacy outside of marriage between one man and one woman, abandoning that commitment is a withdrawal from the faith, triggering a breach of contract argument on behalf of the university.

The questions continue. If Universities Canada members are permitted to use faith tests in hiring personnel, are they permitted to use them in recruiting students? Can they sometimes part company with employees and students if they fall short of commitments in the test? Do we hearken back to the College of Teachers case and draw a line between belief and practice? These and other questions will continue to test UC's membership criteria, and its policy on academic freedom.[40] Division in the commons on the scope of religious freedom is not over.

The broader question that Universities Canada may face in years to come relates to the law of unintended consequences. If many or all faith-based institutions are required to withdraw from the organization, a backlash in the name of freedom of religion is foreseeable, and its impact could be substantial. Comparison can be made to the emerging reaction to policies or behaviours that are seen to diminish freedom of expression. The idea of withdrawing funding from universities that won't defend free speech against attempts to curb it is gaining some attention in the United States,[41] and Canada's Parliament was divided about whether Motion 103 on Islamophobia was about free speech or curbing prejudice against Moslems.[42] The message for all of us resides in labelling differences that are unlikely to go away. What Universities Canada sees as anti-discrimination will continue to be seen by many as clamping down on religious freedom. It is for this reason that we should hope that the Supreme Court of Canada in the TWU case turns away from the balancing of rights (or competing rights) approach in favour of a delineation of the meaning, reach, and limits of freedom of religion in a multicultural, multi-faith society.

Making the World a Better Place: The Social Responsibility of Canadian Universities

Reflections upon the role of universities often begin with an obeisant nod to their enduring success, and a citation of Clark Kerr's observation that most of the Western institutions in existence five hundred years ago that survive today are universities.[1] This insight is quoted in countless university presidential installation addresses and other celebratory speeches about institutions that have increased in number from fewer than one hundred in the Europe of 1500 CE to about twenty thousand worldwide (ninety-seven in Canada) at the present time.

The explanation for this success is a mission that remains current through the ages. Universities exist to develop the human intellect, to enable discernment and the search for truth, and to resist ignorance, intellectual laziness, and coercion. They address needs in the human experience that are constant – not limited in time or episodic – and so we are inclined to forecast a future for them that is as enduring as their past.

A celebration of the perseverance of universities over centuries must acknowledge the change they have experienced. In addition to being more numerous, today's universities are larger by multiples and more complex than their predecessors, with bureaucratic capacity to match. They have different sponsorship, broader curricula, and wider access. They are needed more than ever because the consequences, for individuals and their societies, of forgoing advanced learning are dire now, compared to what they were in industrial and pre-industrial times.

And they have more social responsibilities. These are evident, first, in their regulatory environment. If we explore the A–Z directory on any Canadian university website, we glimpse the modern and regulated university world: animal care, disability services, discrimination, harassment, investment, research protocols and ethics, risk management, insurance, safety, and sustainability – the list goes on. Regulatory regimes abound and require non-academic professional employees in numbers comparable to academic personnel.

Their increased social responsibilities are evident, too, in their accountabilities. Universities may never have been the remote ivory towers of mythology, but the ties that bind them to governments, other funders, partners, and multiple communities have increased in number, and with them come new expectations. In particular, governments have become more intrusive and more demanding in terms of reports, plans, expected priorities, and alignment with other actors within a post-secondary system.

Universities have social responsibilities to nurture and sustain democracy, and to connect to their communities in ways that improve them. George Fallis addresses the first of these in calling for recognition of universities as "integral institutions of liberal democracy."[2] He is not here speaking of their internal governance, egalitarian as opposed to elite standards, or alignment with "progressive" causes. He is locating universities among the institutions required by democratic countries with "an explicit mission to contribute to democratic life."[3] He had in mind larger, more complex, multifaceted institutions – multiversities – but his observations extend to universities in general. He cites Robert Dahl's concern that traditional institutions of primary and secondary education, the media, political parties, and interest groups are insufficient to equip citizens for effective political participation in an age of globalization, increased complexity of issues, and the communications revolution. "The role for the [university] is clear: it can enhance the older institutions and provide new means for civic education, political participation, information and deliberation."[4] The university builds on what Amy Gutman described as a responsibility of primary and secondary education to develop democratic character,[5] but the "fundamental democratic purpose of a university is protection against the tyranny of ideas. Control of the creation of ideas – whether by a majority or a minority – subverts democracy."[6]

"As institutional sanctuaries for free scholarly enquiry, universities can help prevent such subversion. They can provide a realm where new and unorthodox ideas are judged on their intellectual merits, where the men and women who defend such ideas are not strangers but valuable members of the community. Universities thereby serve democracy as sanctuaries of non-repression."[7]

Fallis addresses community connection too – at least in part – when he acknowledges the evolution of the idea of the university "as an institution of the economy, bringing together a new way of thinking about the university and a new way of thinking about the economy."[8] The role of universities in economic development is now explicit, well known, and entails both opportunities and risks. But community connection is about more than the economy. It is also about the multidimensional social and cultural connections between universities and their communities. These connections may be mainly local, as they are for some institutions, or they may have broader, even global reach as they have for internationally competitive multiversities.

We may pause here to acknowledge that previous chapters of this book raise concerns about the capacity of our universities to meet these social responsibilities. The threatened demotion of freedom of expression from paramount value to one among others; positioning rather than debate on differences in the commons; ignorance about governance and attempts to bend it to particular agendas; universities overtaken by a rush to judgment and bypassing the reasoned debate that should be a hallmark of their existence; and tolerance for some discrimination in the commons, should lead us to question whether our universities are the "sanctuaries of non-repression" to which Fallis refers.

Universities must walk a fine line between their social responsibilities and the alignment with causes. They must be hospitable and encouraging to debate, dissent, and their peaceful expressions, while avoiding commitment to the views or causes they represent.

They are sometimes pressured, internally or externally, to take a stand on an issue of the day,[9] but if and when they do, they make a pronouncement on truth and thereby compromise its search. This is contrary to the free and open enquiry for which they exist. Universities enable students and faculty members to make commitments to ideas and to causes, but they must avoid institutional alignment with them. It is not an easy line to walk. University presidents have tried, though they are not in agreement on their speaking notes. Former Princeton president William Bowen observed, "The job of the college president is not to pronounce on the big public issues of the day. The job of the president is to pronounce on educational issues and to lead the academy."[10] The contrary view is that "contributing to the larger public conversation on critical issues" is "part and parcel of their role both as college/university presidents and in the years thereafter."[11] If the latter view is preferred, it must be clear that there is a difference between speaking out on issues other than educational ones, and speaking for the university on them.

Close to the top of the current list of big or critical issues for Canadian universities is a major imperative of the twenty-first century: post-secondary education for Aboriginal students.[12] Indigenous peoples make up about 4 per cent of Canada's population, with larger percentages in some regions and provinces than in others. They are apportioned among approximately six hundred bands (First Nations) and three thousand reserves. It is a younger demographic than the non-Aboriginal population, and growing numbers are urbanized and living off-reserve. There are reported to be more than sixty Aboriginal languages in twelve language families. It is clear that the contemporary Indigenous experience is expressed in many communities, most of them small, increasingly in urban Canada, and in several languages.

Few Aboriginals ventured into the university commons before the past quarter-century. The few who did saw or were taught little of themselves, but this has been changing. Indigenous leaders have recognized education as "the new buffalo"[13] and want their people to have access to the commons, to experience their own images in their learning, and to be successful there. This goal is shared with our universities, and some institutions have been working on this agenda for years; now it is a priority for nearly all of them. The *Report of the Truth and Reconciliation Commission*[14] will be a further catalyst in this effort.

This commission was described by former prime minister Harper as a "cornerstone" of the 2007 Indian Residential Schools Agreement.[15] Reconciliation begins with acknowledgment of the destruction caused to Aboriginal peoples over centuries by newcomers to this land,[16] and with resolution to do everything possible to address its present legacy in the interests of a better future for all Canadians. Shortly after the commission was established, Mr Harper rose in the House of Commons, summarized the history of residential schools, and stated, "The Government of Canada sincerely apologizes and asks the forgiveness of the Aboriginal peoples of this country for failing them so profoundly."[17]

The commission's report must be read in full to appreciate its potential implications for Canada, all levels of government, public and private institutions, and other agencies. Among its ninety-four calls to action is one that would, if acted upon, incorporate the United Nations Declaration on the Rights of Indigenous Peoples into Canadian law and public policy.[18] This means that the declaration must be read in conjunction with the *TRC Report* to understand the policy direction to which both documents point: some compelling proposals, others that are debatable, still others that are highly contentious for constitutional and other reasons.[19] Calls by Prime Minister Trudeau for the implementation in full of both the *TRC Report* and UN Declaration[20] should be deferred in favour of considering TRC calls to action on their individual merits and as they might apply in different settings.

We have seen that the report is not a fresh point of departure for our universities. The areas requiring attention are set out in the most comprehensive written response to date. In early 2017 a University of Toronto committee entrusted with advising the president and provost of the university on the report pointed to five areas needing attention: space, recruitment of faculty and staff, curriculum and co-curriculum initiatives, research ethics and community relations, and institutional leadership and implementation.[21]

The report recognized that "space was central to the indigenous experience at the university"[22] and called for dedicated Indigenous spaces on all three of the U of T's campuses. Naming appropriate spaces in Indigenous languages, displays of more Indigenous public art, and the accommodation of smudging ceremonies in ventilation systems in new construction and renovations were included in the report's calls to action at the University of Toronto.

Many universities now have dedicated Indigenous spaces, some in buildings that have been especially constructed for the purpose: First Peoples House at the University of Victoria, UBC's First Nations Longhouse, and the Gordon Oakes Red Bear Student Centre at the University of Saskatchewan are three examples, and there are more.

Recruitment of Indigenous faculty and staff is a short- and long-term issue, but success beyond the incremental progress that has been made to date requires immediate steps to develop or expand a pool from which qualified appointments can be made. The University of Toronto committee suggested that targeted hiring be considered, Indigenous participation in Indigenous hiring decisions be explored, networking opportunities for current Indigenous employees be created, and holding exit interviews for those who leave. The committee also suggested the inclusion of issues relating to Indigenous peoples in anti-discrimination materials for hiring committees and further effort devoted to ensure cultural awareness. Consideration of an Indigenous advisory council made up of members of external Aboriginal communities, and expanded use of elder services were among remaining suggestions. It will be important, too, for undergraduate Indigenous students with excellent academic records to be encouraged to continue on to graduate studies, and to be supported in that undertaking, in order to develop the pool of candidates qualified for academic appointment.

Indigenous curriculum is the third subject explored, and here the U of T committee made three calls to action: integrate Indigenous content into the curriculum, provide Indigenous learning opportunities for the university's faculty and staff, and work to expand offerings in Aboriginal languages. The committee steered clear of the more prescriptive calls to action on curriculum in the

TRC Report. In particular the commission called upon medical and nursing schools to require all students to take a course dealing with Aboriginal health issues, including the history and legacy of residential schools, the United Nations Declaration on the Rights of Indigenous Peoples, treaties and Aboriginal rights, and Indigenous teachings and practices.[23] Law schools, and journalism and media programs, would require their students to take a course on the history of Aboriginal peoples, including the history and legacy of residential schools, the UN Declaration on the Rights of Indigenous Peoples, treaties and Aboriginal rights, Indigenous law, and Aboriginal-Crown relations.[24] Apart from questions about proposed content – for example why medical and nursing students must be schooled in the UN Declaration – the issue of compulsory courses in principle must be considered.

We must first acknowledge that the mission of a particular university, or the nature of one of its programs, may be such that compulsory instruction on Indigenous issues or perspectives is an appropriate academic requirement. Tribal colleges in the United States are one example, and First Nations University, an institution federated with the University of Regina and specializing in Indigenous knowledge, another. An example of a specialized program within a mainstream university in which such content is academically required is Lakehead University's law school, which has three mandates, one of which is Aboriginal and Indigenous Law.[25]

But the wider prescription of courses and course content raises several questions. Universities already recognize historical neglect of Aboriginal narratives and issues and, in the case of law schools, have included revised content in many courses, including specialized ones focused on Aboriginal law itself. Medical and nursing programs are changing to more fully reflect health issues of Aboriginal peoples. More Indigenous content in curricula is a welcome appeal, but prescribing courses as compulsory on other than academic grounds is not an idea to be embraced. It raises issues about rationale, academic freedom with respect to content and perspectives, and about who should teach what.

Notwithstanding reasons for hesitancy, some leaders and institutions have committed themselves to compulsory education on

Aboriginal issues. Carolyn Bennett, Canada's minister of Indigenous and northern affairs, endorsed the idea for all university students,[26] and it has been under consideration by others. Lakehead University requires an eighteen-hour component committed to Aboriginal content to be embedded within one of the compulsory courses in all student programs. The University of Winnipeg requires all of its students to undertake a full Aboriginal studies course in order to graduate. The question is fairly asked: if compulsory programming is mandated for reasons other than disciplinary or professional competence, why start and stop here? We might argue in favour of compulsory university courses to address woeful ignorance of Canadian history and public affairs, to understand the requirements of sustainability, to develop inter-cultural sensitivity to immigration, to promote global peace, or for other reasons.

If the idea of compulsory programming appeals, it may be seen as a short leap to mandate its content and perhaps the perspectives that must be brought to bear on content. If a course is prescribed to achieve social as distinct from academic goals, we must satisfy ourselves that those goals are reflected in teaching, course readings, and outcomes. The trail may lead to determinations of content that are incompatible with academic freedom, or to a conclusion that only those committed to the social goals should teach the courses. Perhaps only Indigenous instructors should teach them, or at least they should be preferred. If non-Aboriginal instructors are assigned to the course, should they have sensitivity training in addition to academic qualifications to ensure their suitability for the assignment?

The TRC call upon post-secondary institutions to create degree and diploma programs in Aboriginal languages[27] may also be problematic. We have seen that in Canada, there are more than sixty languages in twelve language families. In which of these should degree and diploma programs be offered? What priority should be accorded to them in comparison to instruction in international languages? An issue for universities, as for other organizations, is identifying priorities for which money will be spent. In doing so they must ask whether there would be demand for degree and diploma programs in Aboriginal languages that would support their development and staffing. Perhaps there would be in our largest universities, or those in close proximity to large Aboriginal communities. The point is that academic programs are established to meet sustainable demand, and we do not know the demand here.

It may be that extension and outreach will provide the most practical opportunities for universities to work with Indigenous communities to revitalize and preserve their languages. The University of Victoria's continuing studies program is an excellent example, offering "a comprehensive portfolio of programs in a range of academic disciplines ... to serve adult, part-time, international and geographically dispersed students."[28] Among them is a certificate in Aboriginal Language Revitalization, which includes among its anticipated outcomes the recognition of the role of language in cultural and community sustainability, the identification of language preservation issues and needs, development of strategies to record, document, and revitalize language, and to provide the knowledge foundation for language revitalization work, language and culture teacher education, or heritage/culture professions.[29]

Research ethics and community relations is the fourth subject identified by the University of Toronto committee. The calls to action directed to this subject reflect its sensitivity. "The experience of Indigenous Peoples is that arrangements for the production, collection, ownership and sharing of knowledge and information, are often not satisfactory, and that the benefits of research rarely accrue to them."[30] To address this experience, the committee proposed cultural and research training for scholars intending to work in Indigenous communities, consideration of the development of a research ethics board focused solely on Indigenous-related research, and working with granting councils and other universities to consider the application of the Tri-Council Policy Statement: Ethical Conduct for Research Involving Humans to Indigenous Peoples and Communities.[31]

The U of T committee also reflected upon the leadership required to effect its calls to action. It recognized the commitment and investment necessary for the changes proposed and concluded that the president's and provost's personal leadership will be required, and progress should be monitored by an advisory council with senior leaders from the university with Indigenous membership from within and beyond the university. The discussions contemplated by this committee will no doubt be replicated in universities across the country. Some will be further ahead than others, but the greatest promise for success for all will depend on maintaining a focus on the seventh TRC call to action: "We call upon the federal government to develop with Aboriginal groups a joint strategy to eliminate educational and employment gaps between Aboriginal and non-Aboriginal Canadians." This will require the attention of government, industry and business, and post-secondary leaders for the foreseeable future, and it must not be compromised by uncertainty about relationships in the future.[32] The commons beckons to all Indigenous peoples who can succeed in post-secondary education, and they must not be let down.

To this point our account has addressed the need for a more inclusive commons. We turn our attention now to movements in the name of social responsibility to turn away from some of its activities. At any one time, universities have millions, hundreds of millions, or billions of dollars to invest, and what they do with such large amounts of money naturally attracts interest. Most of the present attention is focused on investments in fossil fuel industries, and organized voices are calling on universities to end them.

This disinvestment campaign has spread across Canada. In Halifax, the students of Dalhousie University formed Divest Dal in 2013 with three goals: more information about the university's investments, a freeze on new investments in fossil fuel and extractive industries, and withdrawal from current investments in them. The organization received the unanimous endorsement of the Dalhousie Student Union and support from the executive of the faculty association, and prepared to petition the university's board of governors.[33] Divest Dal representatives made their case at a board meeting and a separate meeting of the board's investment committee in February 2014. That committee assisted the board in conducting a review of the divestment plea and, late in the same year, it was rejected with a statement from the chair outlining the reasons.[34] He first acknowledged Dalhousie's investments of $45 million in campus sustainability projects with a resulting 20 per cent reduction in greenhouse gas emissions over five years. Citing the board's fiduciary duties, the wishes of its benefactors, and other considerations, the chair concluded, "The board accepts the recommendation of [the investment committee] that Dalhousie not divest assets in carbon-holding companies."[35]

The board decision in November 2014 did not conclude the matter. The university's Senate established a committee to further investigate the issue, one focused on individual companies. In April 2015, some students and others protested a student training contract between Dalhousie and Shell Oil by raising a "Shellhousie" flag and by denouncing the university's president for "prioritizing the interests of a rogue industry at the expense of a sustainable future" for the university. Student leaders of Divest Dal promised to continue their efforts: "If the Board of Governors thought we would go away after November, they were wrong."[36]

Divest Dal is joined by divestment campaigns at more than thirty other universities in Canada. The themes are common ones: divestment petitions that are categorical in their terms, and condemnation of university leaders who do not accede to their demands for lack of either principle or courage, or both.

Pleas to do the right thing are more complicated. The money is not the universities' to deal with as they wish. Their investment portfolios consist mostly of pension funds and endowments, and both carry responsibilities and expectations that must be respected. With the former, investment policy must be aligned with commitments to present and future pensioners, and with solvency and other rules applicable to them. With the latter, it must honour the purposes for which donors made their contributions, and be managed so as to meet the purposes for which endowments are established. Harvard president Drew Faust reminds us that the endowment "is a resource, not an instrument to impel social or political change."[37]

University investments are determined through a framework that is part of university governance. Responsibility rests with a finance or other committee to oversee investments subject to approval of the board of governors. Professional investment advisors work with university staff to develop a portfolio that best meets a university's needs and goals, and that portfolio is reviewed and adjusted on an ongoing basis. Socially responsible and ethical investing are part of an investment framework, and divestment advocates can weigh in with their views, as can others. The University of British Columbia offers a compelling example of a modern university investment framework that explicitly provides for divestment potential.

UBC has a wholly owned subsidiary (UBC Investment Management Trust, or IMANT) to provide comprehensive investment management of the university's endowment, pension, working capital, and other funds, a portfolio of nearly $4 billion. It also has an Endowment Responsible Investment Policy, established in 2013, and a committee charged with advising the board's finance committee on responsible investments. Those sitting on this committee include three members of the Board of Governors that have been elected, respectively, by faculty, staff, and students. Its terms of reference charge the committee with reviewing responsible investment proposals from students, faculty, staff, and alumni. The committee entertains divestment proposals supported by a case that demonstrates:

A proven and overwhelming social, political, economic or environmental rationale supported by a body that is widely seen as competent and objective;

Reasonable evidence that divestment is seen as the best way to achieve the desired outcome;

Illustration that the request is consistent with its other University relationships or a further argument to align other University academic activities with the request;

The demonstration of a lack of alternative policies as effective at a lower cost or more effective at the same cost;

Consistency with the University's legal obligations as trustee.[38]

Few Canadian universities have investment portfolios the size of UBC's, but the above criteria for entertaining divestment pleas could be received by all of them as a responsible approach to the challenges they present.

There are other issues with divestment campaigns. They treat all actors within a target industry or activity in the same way, and without acknowledgment that some may be a positive influence both in their own behaviours and in influencing others. They also overlook the possibility that large investors may have more influence over the behaviour of entities in which they have an interest by remaining invested rather than by walking away. Whether or not these objections are substantive or compelling must be determined case by case. They were not in one of history's most prominent disinvestment campaigns – Anti-Apartheid – where there was an absolute. The evil of racial suppression was the target, amelioration was not a credible goal, abolition was the only answer. In the anti-tobacco campaign, it could be said that massive health risks of smoking with no compensating health benefits point to abolition, but here the choice of smokers to smoke must also be respected, and so the tobacco industry survives, though with regulation that seeks to limit its harms to adults for whom the risks are known and tolerable.

There is no absolute in the present case. We humans need energy for our activities, and there is no compelling evidence that we would have it in sufficient quantities without carbon-producing industries. There are alternatives – solar, nuclear, wind – though for the present they are seen as supplementing carbon sources, not replacing them. Here we are into comparisons, and so industries or actors that engage in best environmental practices and research into ameliorating harmful consequences are to be encouraged, making blanket condemnation – and divestment – inadvisable.

There are other targets for banishment from the commons. Genetically modified organisms, particularly those used in the production of food, have been the subject of divestment initiatives. Food Democracy Now[39] and others inspired by the divestment campaign aimed at fossil fuels[40] have called for divestment – aimed particularly at Monsanto, in their view the corporate embodiment of all they fear or dislike about GMOs and agricultural biotechnology in general. There is more sociology than science underlying the appeal. GMOs are associated by some with a transformation of farming and the rural landscape in ways that produce a mixture of anxiety and nostalgia. Universities with large agricultural establishments are familiar with debates about both the science and sociology of GMOs, and they are ongoing.

In their distinct settings these accounts enlighten us on the importance of inclusion of Indigenous peoples and cultures in the commons, and they caution us about divestment campaigns. But what do they say about the nature and limits of the social obligations of our universities? We begin by reminding ourselves that we use the word *university* in different senses, variably as a single entity, a collegial forum, or a collection of individuals. They are not discrete categories; individuals may participate in one, two, or all three of them, and their responsibilities differ from one to another. It is important, however, that in any one context we understand the particular meaning we attribute to *university*.

It is in the first sense that the word is used here. In law, universities are corporate entities; for many important activities their behaviours and accountabilities are identified as those of a single entity. Acting in the name of the university is a solemn undertaking and it is reserved for only a few of its senior officers. As members of a collegial forum, or as individuals in the commons, they may have different or more nuanced opinions than those they express in the university's name, and their opinions may not prevail in the many contests of ideas in those settings. But whatever their views, when their statements are prefaced by the words "on behalf of the university" they speak authoritatively for the university. There are many voices in the university, but as a single entity, it speaks with one only.

It is for this reason that we must discuss the social obligations of universities with circumspection, and with an eye on the reasons for their establishment and endurance. The pursuit of social justice is not among them. It is important that we believe that the arduous searches for truth and meaning that are undertaken in the commons will better reveal the meaning of social justice and enable progress in its pursuit. However, it is not for the university to declare the search over, the truth identified, the meaning of social justice revealed, and the path for its attainment determined. If it did so it would reveal itself to be a political organization, one vulnerable to the vicissitudes of political life, including an uncertain fate as the winds of politics shift and change.

This argument does not imply that universities are freed from the obligation to be just. On the contrary, they should strive to do justice in employment matters, in how they treat students, in their exchanges with communities, and in how they behave in discharging their responsibilities. It is here – how they behave – that the line between doing justice and pursuing social justice becomes less distinct. A university's quest for the success of Indigenous students, accessibility generally, and sustainability intersects with important societal goals and may lead to a convergence of them in the commons. But here is the point. Whether shared or not, it is the university's goals qua university to which, as a single entity, it must be committed. A broader diffusion of beliefs, values, commitments, and goals will exist in the commons and will compete for attention and impact. Some may align with university goals, others will not.

There will always be claimants in the commons who would urge the elevation of their views on the issues of the day to university policy and beyond, to a social justice agenda that would be binding on all. The university as single entity must be highly selective in identifying and pursuing its social responsibilities and must be able to relate them to its mission and raison d'être, and here we conclude as we began this chapter. Universities exist to develop the human intellect, to enable discernment and the search for truth, and to resist ignorance, intellectual laziness, and coercion. Their most important social responsibility is to do this, and to do it well.

chapter seven

Conclusion

If preceding chapters bear out the title claim that we are in a divided university commons, our next task is to reflect upon what has taken us here and where we go next. We should not assume that remedial action would widely be seen as necessary. Are these differences not simply part of life in institutions perceived by the public as being somewhat unruly? Do they not feature the normal push and pull, give and take, of the contentiousness that is common in academic life? Canadian universities in general are academically sound; some are very good and a few are great. What's to worry? All is good, or as good as it gets.

Before moving on with a complacent shrug we should remind ourselves about the kinds of divisions we see revealed in the analysis to date. Chapter 1 took us into the commons at the University of British Columbia in which we witnessed a struggle about academic freedom and university governance, a costly one in terms of reputations, time, and money. In chapter 2 we crossed the country and entered the commons at Dalhousie, where hundreds of thousands of dollars were spent in a crisis that rocked the university and threatened the futures of many people. In chapter 3 we found ourselves on several campuses to experience the decline of freedom of expression from paramount value to a competing one. In chapter 4 we arrived at Carleton University to revisit academic freedom and governance in a case that disrupted its board for an extended period of time. In chapter 5 we moved on to Trinity Western where discrimination in the commons is defended in the name of religious freedom. And in chapter 6 we reflected upon the social responsibilities of universities, and upon emergent challenges to universities in meeting them.

These are not matters to be airily dismissed as routine business. They touch upon issues that are central to the reasons why universities exist, and the ways in which they are organized to protect their independence and integrity. Our universities are vital institutions and we diminish them, or allow them to be diminished, at our peril. And so the cases and examples documented here rightly command our attention and demand coherent answers to the challenges they present.

We may proceed by identifying the themes that emerge from the discussion in previous chapters, and the first of these is governance. It is now a half-century since the last major report on Canadian university governance was completed. Bicameralism did not originate with the Duff-Berdahl Report[1] but was affirmed in it with important modifications. "It was the Flavelle Commission of 1906 which clearly articulated the rationale and framework for bicameralism."[2] To protect university autonomy there would be two bodies. "The public interest in this internal decision making process should be delegated to a corporate board composed of government appointed citizens, and this board should assume responsibility for administrative policy. Academic matters would be the responsibility of a senate, composed primarily of members of the academic community. Bicameralism can therefore be seen as an attempt to balance public and academic interests within the formal, corporate governance structures of the university."[3]

In the years following the Flavelle Commission, the model it proposed was widely adopted across Canada,[4] though it was not long before faculty and students complained of insufficient influence, particularly with their boards. "Faculty and student constituencies argued that their interests were not being appropriately considered or represented in the university governance process. The governing board was viewed by these constituencies as isolated from the ethos of academic work since it was composed largely of businessmen. The governance process was viewed as secretive, since board and senate meetings were seldom open to the public, and dominated by business or corporate interests, rather than the interests of faculty and students."[5]

Duff and Berdahl did not abandon bicameralism but they "encouraged universities to create more open, transparent governance arrangements, including faculty participation on the university governing board."[6]

This happened, with substantial numbers of faculty and students joining boards, and with larger numbers of students on senates. The changes were not limited to boards and senates but extended into deliberative processes at all levels, including the composition of presidential search committees. No longer the exclusive responsibility of governing boards, the appointment of presidents rested with committees, with representation from internal and external constituencies making recommendations to boards that usually felt obliged to accept them, whether with enthusiasm or not. Also senate and many board meetings became public. Queen's principal J.A. Corry summarized what he thought to be the cumulative impact of the changes: "much of the substance of power has been taken out of the president's office and away from the board of governors. The members of the academic staff now have what has been taken out, and they have nearly a veto on what is left."[7]

These developments to increase faculty and student presence in governance were soon followed by one of even greater significance. University faculty associations were beginning to make the transition to faculty unions certified under provincial trade union legislation – not at all institutions, for some of our best universities resisted the move – but over time at most Canadian universities.[8] This development has had a profound impact on university governance as faculty unions sought to acquire academic authority through collective bargaining. They have been successful in their quest to the point that some in their national organization – the Canadian Association of University Teachers – see them as being more important to the future of university governance than senates.[9]

Other changes were converging. Universities were growing in size and taking on the responsibilities incurred by a more regulated environment. Governments were paying more attention to them, and with their attention came more demands. Responding to the new realities required more managerial ways that were an uneasy fit with academic culture. The stage was set for a new round of governance controversy.

Cases examined in this book must be considered in this context. What lessons are to be drawn, in particular from the Jennifer Berdahl and Root Gorelick episodes, for university governance as it has evolved fifty years after the Duff-Berdahl Report? We remind ourselves of three risks that materialized in the Berdahl case: first, the vulnerability of boards to attacks upon their integrity to which they are circumscribed in responding; second, the tendency of faculty associations to resort quickly and publicly to adversarialism; and third, the absence of others – faculty, senate members, or the media – who could bring balance to discussion on the public record. In the Gorelick case we are reminded of these as well, and in addition, we note the consequences of ignorance about university governance, even on the part of those who have spent their professional lives in the academy.

The Berdahl case is a story of governance vulnerability. The professor publicly denounced board members, corporately and by implication individually, for being racist and sexist, and for disadvantaging their sitting president on account of his appearance. For reasons that are well understood by careful observers of governance, her targets were reluctant to reply to these accusations, leaving them susceptible to the negative conclusions drawn from unanswered public allegations. The faculty association rallied to Berdahl's side and launched its own campaign to discredit the board. Its reach within UBC, combined with the absence of rebuttal to its allegations, meant that securing non-confidence votes was easy. The nearly complete public silence of other voices at UBC contributed to the result. Most faculty did not vote on the confidence motions, and few of their voices were raised in public to protest unfolding events; the university senate was largely absent from the controversy. The problem was compounded by the media, whose superficial coverage of the issues did little to inform the public about what was occurring at one of the country's leading universities. And government had little choice but to look on with concern lest it be condemned for interfering in university affairs.

At Carleton University some of the same issues surfaced. The misclassification of the issue as one of academic freedom; the rallying of the faculty union, other Carleton unions, and the Canadian Association of University Teachers to Gorelick's side; the vulnerability of the board to their attacks; the silence of others who might have brought wiser counsel to the differences: all were present here. Joining them was a demonstration of unfamiliarity with the requirements of good governance that can only be described as startling. Gorelick, his union, other Carleton unions, and the Canadian Association of University Teachers saw the issues as academic freedom and free speech only.

It is time to revisit the reports of the Flavelle Commission and Messrs Duff and Berdahl, and to ask whether bicameralism persists as an appropriate model of governance, given the changes since these reports were commissioned. This would require a study, one that engages the academy with governments and other interested parties, in a broadly based consideration of best governance practices for Canadian universities in the twenty-first century. Its terms of reference should renew the Flavelle/Duff-Berdahl debate on whether the public interest is adequately accommodated in contemporary governance bodies and practices. Its focus should be on protecting university autonomy in decision-making but within a framework that makes repetition of cases like Berdahl and Gorelick improbable. Legislated change in the wake of such a study would be a likely prospect, and so it is important that provincial governments be connected to the work in ways that see its results implemented.

We shall return to this subject at the conclusion of this chapter, but we should first revisit some of the other themes that emerge from the preceding discussion.

A lack of robust debate in places where we would expect it to occur is another of them, and there are many contributing factors. We have seen that the sidetracking of governance bodies is part of the explanation. A tendency to rush to judgment; protagonists with a Manichaean view of differences; processes that are preordained to reach a particular result[10] all play a role. So does a lack of informed media coverage.

Reference has already been made to this problem in the Berdahl case. In the Dalhousie example, the local media appeared to have been won over early to the cause of discipline. Days after the story broke, the Halifax newspaper concluded that the university administration should "act independently and immediately to investigate the Facebook record and to determine who posted what." And "it should suspend, expel or otherwise seriously discipline" the individuals involved.[11]

Little attention was devoted to restorative justice alternatives, and what was said on the subject too often left the impression that they were soft, touchy-feely options that would let the Facebook group members off lightly.

It may be that financial and other pressures on the conventional media make it more difficult to deploy the resources necessary for investigative journalism. Whatever the reason, it is difficult to follow the media accounts of the cases and examples in previous chapters without disappointment in the quality of reporting and analysis. We understand that it is controversy that attracts readers and listeners, and the fact of controversy will dominate reports, but context and reasons matter too, and we do not see or hear much of these. The universities themselves bear some of the responsibility; they need to be more proactive in visits to newspaper editorial boards and in holding media briefings. University leaders must become better at telling their sides of the stories.

Concern about the quality of conventional media coverage is compounded by the social media. "In recent years, the capacity of increasingly powerful, small mobile devices has created an almost addictive connection between users and their online links. The Internet upended the business model for traditional media, and a worrisome outcome of this trend has been the decline of investigative journalism and the difficulties people encounter in trying to assess reliable versus unreliable sources of information."[12]

Social media access of ill-informed and intemperate voices to audiences, sometimes large ones, is a familiar problem now. What is not yet clear is their role in inciting others and influencing outcomes. We are reminded that soon after news of Dalhousie's Facebook group broke, an online petition calling for their expulsion attracted 50,000 names, and a related one attracted an additional 45,000 signatures. We cannot be certain of their role in causing early opinion to run against President Florizone's preference for restorative justice over discipline, but it appears that at least they contributed to a heightened anxiety, even fervour, about unfolding events. Does this contribute to the rush to judgment we see so often in our examples? Does it increase the risk of mistakes and poor decisions? We don't know, but we should be troubled by the possibility that the answer is yes.

We should not leave this subject without recalling the particular responsibility of universities to illuminate problems, to describe them accurately, and to seek the best truth possible in their resolution. This responsibility should weigh on the shoulders of all in the commons. It should also lead universities to consider their adaptation to a new world in which they must improve and speed up their own communications so as to better compete in the new and rapidly changing marketplace of ideas.

Academic freedom is a prominent theme in any discussion of universities. It is a core value in the academy, just as judicial independence is in the administration of justice, or the Hippocratic Oath in the practice of medicine. To be a core value it must be widely understood and accepted within and beyond the academy, and in its most important dimensions it is. No one challenges its centrality to teaching and research. It is when academic freedom is claimed in a wider sphere of activity that there is ambiguity and possible dispute. In our cases and examples we have seen academic freedom violations claimed by Jennifer Berdahl at UBC, Michael Persinger at Laurentian, Jordan Peterson at University of Toronto, and Root Gorelick at Carleton. In this writer's opinion two of the claims (those of Persinger and Peterson) are compelling, and the remaining two are not. But the significance here does not lie in one person's opinion; it lies in the definitional ambiguity that could produce this divide. We have seen some of the reasons for this in chapter 4. Among them are negotiated extensions that bring criticism of the university or its leadership under the protection of academic freedom, and the open-ended statement that stipulates what CAUT believes to be included within its ambit but avoids any commitment on its limits or concomitant responsibilities.

The choice in the commons is a simple one. Let the ambiguity persist along with its inevitable disputes, or attempt to arrive at a statement to which both Universities Canada and CAUT can sign on. It would not solve all issues, but there would be progress in reasoning from a common base, and a greater likelihood that all in the commons could explain to a sometimes incredulous public what academic freedom is, what it is not, and why it should matter to everyone.

There remain two aspects of this subject that require our attention. The first can be dealt with quickly. A consequence of disagreement within the academy about the reach of academic freedom means that difficult cases are remitted to external authorities. The Berdahl case was put before a retired British Columbia Supreme Court judge, and it may be that our remaining examples will be determined by arbitrators or in the courts. This should not be a welcome development in institutions that prize their autonomy. The forum in which academic freedom issues should first be addressed is the university senate. Senates are responsible for academic matters, and academic freedom is one of them. We don't know what the results would have been had the Berdahl and Gorelick cases been remitted to the senates at UBC and Carleton, but it is reasonable to suppose that there would have been debates that would have illuminated issues and potential solutions. Instead we end up with governance controversies at both institutions.

Our final topic in this area is freedom of speech, and it is important to our analysis in two respects. First, it has a relationship to academic freedom that must be clarified, and second, it presages our transition to freedom of expression in general, one of the most important subjects of this book. In our earlier comparison of the statements on academic freedom of Universities Canada, the Canadian Association of University Teachers, and the joint AACU/AAUP statement in the United States, we noted the indeterminacy of the CAUT statement. It informs us about what academic freedom includes, though not what it is, and because academic freedom is indeterminate, so too is free speech and the difference between the two.

The argument here is that it is the triumvirate of professorial responsibilities – teaching, research, and service – that invokes academic freedom. When a professor of history is doing history, whether in the classroom, coffee room, home study, or as a guest speaker for a service club, she has academic freedom. And we are glad she does, because it gives us assurance that her professional judgment as a historian is unencumbered by extraneous pressures and constraints. When she turns her attention to commenting on university governance and administration, a claim that she does so with academic freedom is less compelling, though it may prevail because of a collective agreement or other understanding within her institution. Beyond these spheres, the argument continues, academic freedom does not have reach though freedom of speech does, and that is important too, because the work of the academy requires many exchanges apart from those involved in teaching, research, service, and criticizing the president or board of governors. The key difference is that academic freedom confers stronger protection than freedom of speech. The latter may be limited by law, contract, or context, and by the expectation we have for behaviours that facilitate exchanges necessary in the workplace or in everyday life.

This argument explains the approach in this book to the Gorelick case at Carleton University. To conclude on that case, Dr Gorelick has academic freedom when and wherever he is doing biology. The collective agreement at Carleton is not explicit on whether he has it when he criticizes governance and administration, but even if he has, once he joined the university's board of governors, he took on responsibilities that supersede his academic freedom in that context and limit his freedom of speech. Now that he is off the board he has the freedom of speech to say what he likes.

The broader theme of freedom of expression is addressed in chapter 3, and its two conclusions are ominous: freedom of expression

is under attack in our universities; and it is threatened too by a com-
bination of intellectual laziness, ideology, and anger. What would a
campaign to end these threats look like?

It would begin with a re-emphasis on why universities exist,
and a clear statement that freedom of expression is an essential
condition of their existence. It would acknowledge the potential
for discomfort and offence as a result of this freedom and make it
clear that neither is sufficient reason to curb its exercise. It would
warn everyone in the commons that the university will take all
measures necessary to protect the free exchange of ideas, including disciplinary action against those who would deny others their
expression. It would convey the truism that civility facilitates and
promotes freedom of expression, and that the university expects
civil discourse in the commons.

If this was our point of departure, what would our conclusions
be on the examples in chapter 3? Netanyahu and Coulter would
speak, and the rioters who tried to prevent them from doing so
would be held accountable by Concordia and University of Ottawa.
The anti-abortion demonstrators at University of Calgary would
hold their placards facing outward, and those who didn't like
them could look the other way; the partygoers at Brock, U of T, and
Queen's would be vulnerable to criticism for poor judgment in their
selection of costumes, but those who would condemn or punish
them would not find sympathetic ears. The York University mural
depicting Palestinian anger at West Bank Israeli settlement would
remain on display, and the militancy of demonstrators equating
the issue with apartheid in South Africa would attract neither support nor sympathy. The claim that the yoga class at University of
Ottawa was cultural misappropriation would be seen as silly, and
the class would have proceeded without interruption. Laurentian
University professor Michael Persinger would teach his section of
introductory psychology using whatever language he felt would
advance the course goals. University of Toronto Professor Jordan
Peterson would be free to choose his pronouns in his classroom.
Ryerson's Henry Parada would have been free to come and go as
he liked at the anti-racism meeting without incurring the condemnation of the Black Liberation Collective. McGill's Andrew Potter

would not have been criticized in a tweet sent in the name of his university. Three more examples occurred at the time of writing.[13] A concessionaire who had been operating in commercial space at Wilfrid Laurier University's graduate student space was expelled from his premises for a tongue-in-cheek help-wanted ad seeking a "slave" whose pay would be "crap." A scheduled speech at UBC by former CEO of the Vancouver Olympics John Furlong was cancelled (later reinstated) because of forty-year-old sexual assault allegations found to be unsubstantiated; and a St Francis Xavier student protested a guest speaker invitation to Marie Henein, Jian Ghomeshi's defence lawyer who defended him successfully against charges of sexual assault. Clearly, it follows from the foregoing analysis that the concessionaire should not have been expelled, and John Furlong and Marie Henein should have been welcome to speak at UBC and St FX respectively.

It must be conceded that the suggested disposition of particular cases is an easier task than accounting for the phenomenon they cumulatively represent. While there is no explanation applicable to all these examples, there is a recurring theme in many of them, and it is disengagement and passivity on the part of faculty and students. This is partly a function of size. In large institutions it is possible to see much of what happens on campus as remote from the daily concerns of those whose focus is on their academic work. They may not be paying attention to these and similar episodes; if they are, they may wish to avoid engagement with them. In the case of students, they may be juggling their studies and the employment they need to continue their education. It is difficult to believe that large numbers of faculty and students at the universities represented in our examples would have looked upon these episodes with sympathy and support. Many of them may have shared the bewilderment of the general public.

This disengagement is reflected in voting numbers. Relatively few among faculty and students elect leaders of their organizations. And we saw that at UBC most faculty absented themselves from non-confidence motions and efforts to purge the board of some of its members. Did they just not want to be bothered? Did they look upon events with disdain or at least reservations? Were they quietly in agreement and supportive of actions being taken in their name? Unfortunately their stance is not one of neutrality. It effectively cedes voice and influence to the relatively few who present themselves to lead campus organizations. These leaders like to call upon others for accountability, but who holds them accountable if most of their constituents are paying little or no attention?

Freedom of expression is central to our analysis because it is an indispensable condition of the university commons. It also has expanded "to encompass nearly all non-violent forms of expression,"[14] which means that proponents of religious freedom can argue that their beliefs merit the same protection as expressions of other beliefs in the commons. This helps to explain why the leaders of Trinity Western University can argue that their faith covenant is entitled to constitutional protection. It may help us explain, too, why TWU president Bob Kuhn sees challenging the covenant "as a new era of persecution against Christians and their views."[15] His alarm is not well founded, but it is rooted in the idea that TWU is being singled out for discriminatory treatment, and it raises an important question to which we alluded but did not develop in chapter 5. Are all religious beliefs entitled to constitutional protection, with the only issue being the extent of their protection in the balancing of religious freedoms with other rights and freedoms? Remember, here, that the religious belief for which constitutional protection is being sought is one whose practice at TWU is at variance with a constitutionally protected human right. There is a compelling argument[16] that a religious belief at variance with a constitutionally protected human right should not enjoy constitutional protection beyond the beliefs and life choices of its proponents. The belief in question here is that it is wrong to marry someone of the same sex, and the freedom of TWU's faith community to hold that belief, and to conform to it in their private lives, is uncontested. But when the community reaches outward into the public commons and practises its beliefs to the disadvantage of others who enjoy constitutional protection, it reaches the limits of constitutional protection for those beliefs.

And so the TWU controversy should not be conceived as a balancing of religious freedom (which is a good value) and freedom from discrimination (which is another good value). Both the British Columbia and Ontario Courts of Appeal employed this balancing of rights approach, albeit to opposite results. A preferable one might be to recognize that freedom of religion is not engaged here. In moving from its faith-based community to offer education in the public commons, TWU changes arenas from one in which it can practise its discriminatory beliefs to one in which it cannot. Quite simply, its discriminatory religious beliefs should not be in play in the commons.

Underlying this argument is an important difference between freedom of expression and freedom of religion. With the former it is expression itself that is protected; content is immaterial unless contrary to law. With the latter, we are privileging content by according it a special status: the belief itself enjoys constitutional protection because it is an article of religious faith. In a multicultural, multifaith society we should not accord privilege to religious beliefs that are discriminatory by the standards of Canadian society. What do we say of sentiments of some of Islamic faith that women should accept patriarchy and remain in their houses except when necessity compels them to go out? Or about an Imam in Montreal reported to have incited violence against Jews? Do we say these are religious beliefs and therefore protected to the extent that they are not found wanting in the balance with other rights and freedoms? Or should we say that these beliefs enjoy no constitutional protection beyond freedom of expression and perhaps not even that if Canada's hate laws have been violated. The latter, it is suggested, is the preferable view.

We have now reached the point at which we can move the discussion to the level of public policy and to return to the subject of governance in that context.

The existence of our universities and conditions that enable their success are predicated on an understanding of their missions, on confidence that they are well run, and on their accountability for the resources that are made available to them. In general, the story of Canadian universities is one of success because these tests have been met. If we could view the subject matter of this book as quaint examples at variance with a continuing success story, we might note them with interest and pass on to other matters. But if they give us pause about our universities' present direction and values, we are wise to reflect upon their meaning and to ask how they, and we, can do better.

They give us cause for concern because they are suggestive of wavering in mission and values, and instability in governance. If these persist or grow, our universities will be diminished, and so we need assurance that they will not. Some of those in our commons need reminders of their missions and that the central raison d'être for universities – intellectual development, discernment, and maturity – is unchanged. To this have been added layers of responsibilities borne of our needs to educate professionals, meet regulatory requirements, and sustain commitments to many communities. Universities do not exist to pursue social justice or comfort, and they must not have their purpose and activities bent by those more interested in crusades than in the hard work of intellectual life.

Clarity on the purpose and focus of universities is important for all in the commons, but it is a responsibility of university administrations. They are given the task of ensuring that the universities' activities are aligned with societal needs and expectations, and their voices stand apart from the many others in the commons in that they speak for their universities as a whole. They must lead, and despite the many nuances of leadership in this setting, they must be effective in setting direction, tone, and example, and in bridging the many divides in the commons.

Other recent books have been devoted to leadership in the university world.[17] Presidential offices are precarious for several reasons, but they are particularly vulnerable to weak governance. Boards and senates must be effective in order for bicameralism to work and for leaders to concentrate on the most important duties affecting their universities. Canadians and their governments should take note of the cases and examples in this book and should ask a number of questions: Have changes in universities over the past half-century imposed strains on bicameralism that undermine boards and senates in discharging their responsibilities as set out in legislation and charters? Do faculty unions and associations occupy a space that alters bicameralism in material and appropriate respects? Are the sizes and compositions of boards and senates optimal? Is bicameralism, however altered, the best model for the future, or should we contemplate radical change in university governance? Before offering tentative answers to these questions, we should note that they are of such importance that they require a new commission for their study and determination. This is not internal work for the universities themselves. It requires a blue ribbon panel, perhaps initiated by Universities Canada and led by a former Supreme Court justice, and consisting of members well versed in governance including a former university president with a distinguished track record.[18] It should include a senior representative of Canadian provincial governments who can assist in ensuring that legislative changes recommended by the panel are acted upon by them.

Anticipating that a commission of this kind is not a question of "if" but of "when," we can reflect further upon some of the issues that will be before them. On the question of whether boards are struggling with the greater weight of their burdens, the answer is yes. Governance oversight of universities is more complex by reason of their greater size and complexity, and wider regulatory framework. It is also tested by fractiousness, and by uncertainty among their members about whose interests they serve. Whether the greater burden is manageable within the present bicameral framework is a question for further exploration. What we know is that boards or equivalents are an essential guarantor for university autonomy, and it is in everyone's interest that they work well.

Senates face burdens of a different order, and two recent studies[19] illuminate them for us. In the first of these, in 2012 Pennock et al. polled university secretaries on key issues and challenges facing their senates. Of the themes they reported, three stood out that are notable here: "tension between the roles and responsibilities of the senate in relation to the university administration and board within university governance ... issues and challenges associated with the tension between individual and constituency interests versus the interests of the university as a whole ... [and] the challenge of engaging senate members."[20] Responses also pointed to "a gap between the roles that senate does play within the university and the role that it should play"[21] and noted that "the role and responsibilities of the senate need to be clarified."[22]

The second study focused on themes arising from the 2012 survey. "Suggested reforms include: reviewing and improving senate performance; fostering a culture of trust and respect among and within governing bodies; clarifying spheres of authority and accountability; and promoting the importance of collegial governance and oversight within the institution."[23] The authors concluded that collegial governance "can and should be a vehicle for engaged citizenship within the institution"[24] and referenced Donald Kennedy's 1997 observation about the professoriate's declining institutional loyalty: "To the extent that is true, it seems likely that it can only be reversed by the sense of shared responsibility and common purpose that comes from meaningful participation in the institution's future. Surely that is a central part of academic duty, and its restoration will be vital to the re-establishment of the entente cordiale between the University and society."[25]

Shared responsibility and common purpose are not prominent in a commons with divisions, as distinct from differences, or when positioning rather than debate carries the day more often than it should. One of the issues to be addressed in a new governance study would be the conditions necessary to restore or strengthen shared responsibility and common purpose to the commons, and to university governance.

The next question that must be addressed by our prospective commission is whether faculty unions and associations occupy a space that alters bicameralism in material and appropriate respects. The answer, in Canada, on materiality is yes, and on whether appropriate, no.[26] An expansive view on terms and conditions of employment has taken faculty associations into areas that are academic in nature. In its most extreme variant, a Canadian Association of University Teachers discussion paper in 2009 opined that "because academic staff are the effective agents for the execution of the research and educational functions of the academy our working environment and our terms and conditions of employment are inseparable from academic policies and objectives. Academic staff have a legal entitlement to engage in the collective bargaining of all their terms and conditions of employment."[27] More ominous is a CAUT policy statement that declares "that the Board and Senate should operate within the context of procedures and rules set out in legislation constituting the institution and in collective agreements negotiated between the institution and its academic staff."[28] Other than providing for boards and senates, legislation is silent on how boards and senates should operate, leaving it to them to establish their own rules and bylaws. Here the CAUT policy statement claims a superintending role over boards and senates, the precise domain of which is to be determined through collective bargaining. CAUT's president recently referred to this superintending role in asserting, "We need to protect the collegial role of our members by building provisions into our collective agreements that clearly set out where boards of governors and senates fit into the picture."[29]

This claim should serve as a warning to university administrations and to provincial governments. It is a reminder to the former of a collective bargaining agenda that must be resisted, and of an urgent need to strengthen senates as the academic voices of our universities. It also serves notice on provincial governments of the CAUT/faculty union view that the governance of public universities must tilt more in the direction of collective bargaining and less in the direction of the governing bodies established by their legislation.

We noted in Berdahl and Gorelick that senates at UBC and Carleton played at most a background role, leaving the initiative to their faculty associations. We can only speculate on what difference there might have been had the senates at both institutions debated the issues of academic freedom at large in these cases, but we might have been able to count on better analysis of those issues, and more constructive dispositions of them. However, with the ambiguity of roles and uncertainty of impact described by Pennock et al., senates are on the defensive and have made concessions on the academic role that has been entrusted to them by legislation. Senates should be reminded that nature abhors a vacuum, and the vacuum they are creating is being filled by faculty unions.

Governments should make it clear to our prospective commission that they will not countenance the hollowing out through
collective bargaining of governance provisions established by
legislation. Where this has already been excessive it should be
rolled back; where it has not it must be resisted. Legislation is
necessary to establish the boundaries between academic governance by senates, and collective bargaining on terms and conditions of employment.

The third question that must be addressed by this commission
takes us to the size and composition of boards and senates. They
vary greatly in size, though in general, efforts to reduce board
numbers have been underway at some universities, while the size
and composition of senates have largely been unchanged since reforms were implemented pursuant to the Duff-Berdahl Report. The
impact of that report is now clear. On the positive side it achieved
what its authors intended – the presence of faculty, staff, and students on boards, and of students on senates. Less positive is the
contribution it made to the emergence of constituencies at board
tables. We noted earlier that other board-governed entities have
less difficulty in identifying their stakeholders; they are the shareholders in publicly trading companies or the relevant community
of interest in not-for-profits. It is not so simple in universities – as
the Gorelick case so clearly demonstrates. Apart from his sense
that he was on the Carleton board to represent his constituents,
others at Carleton thought that the answer to the issues he represented was to adjust numbers to ensure a majority of insiders
– employees and students – on the board. Their message should
not be lost on anyone. It would mean a diminished presence of the
public interest at the board table.

Carleton is not the only illustration of this issue. Recently
University of Montreal rector Guy Breton was condemned by
the university's faculty union for governance reform proposals
that included provision for a majority of external members on the
university's board of governors.[30] As we have seen in chapter 4
of this volume, the rector is wise to seek this change.

Our commission revisiting bicameralism should not proceed
from the assumption that Duff-Berdahl's impact was entirely

positive and the only issues are those that illustrate strains on bi-cameralism that have developed in the interim. It should ask the question whether the independence of universities and the public interest served by their boards and senates are best addressed by bodies composed as they are at present. It should also take note of the CAUT/union view outlined above and prevent its realization. And it should be clear in its insistence on why boards and senates exist and on what their duties are – for all their members.

The last question in this area is whether we can expect to go forward with bicameralism, perhaps with a new round of reforms, or whether a more radical approach to governance might be entertained. Consideration of this issue should include asking whether the University of Toronto's experience with unicameralism is such that other universities might seek to emulate the experience. Established in 1971, the Governing Council oversees the academic, business, and student affairs of the university. It has fifty members, twenty-five from within the university and twenty-five from beyond. In addition to the chancellor and president there are two members of the administrative staff, eight alumni, sixteen government appointees including the chair and vice-chair, six undergraduate students, two graduate students, two presidential appointees, and twelve members of the teaching staff. Would unicameralism at the centre combined with strong academic councils in individual faculties work better than the current bicameral model? Whether this or other possibilities, we must not be complacent about changes needed to ameliorate the pressures on the bicameral model. While more research on the subject is needed, we can forecast change on a considerable scale. If it does not take place our universities may face more radical and less welcome governance reform in the future.

Afterword

We can now appreciate the distinction between differences in the commons and a commons that is divided. Our agora, our marketplace of ideas, celebrates differences because they are what make discussion and debate possible. Our differences lead us to the conditions that make them possible and even productive, and so they are welcome in our commons. A divided commons is in sharp contrast. It features position and exclusion, and may presage expulsion and closure. It carries with it the message that debate is over, or at least unnecessary. Division is the antithesis of the commons.

It is important that we bring a non-judgmental attitude of mind into the commons, not because we are to refrain from making judgments but because of the care with which they must be made. We insist upon evidence, not assumption; reason, not pronouncement; and conclusions supported by both. Our search for truth is arduous and complex, and it is never ending. It is not for us to post a sign at the entrance to the commons proclaiming its closure because truth is revealed. It must always be open.

This book was written because it is feared that its stories herald a divided commons more than they do one with differences. A board chair phones a professor to discuss her condemnation of the board he leads and is pushed from the commons. A rush to judgment in favour of expelling or suspending the student members of a Dalhousie Facebook group threatens to carry the day. Invited speakers are turned away from universities by protesters who seek a safe space in which they will find refuge from unwelcome opinions. A display of abortion images is curtailed when viewers find them offensive. Unwise costume choices are elevated to major infractions. The Israel/Palestine issue is an unbridgeable campus divide. Students with disabilities find that their relief through yoga is also cultural misappropriation. Professors are corrected for their language, or for language attributed to them even when they have not spoken. Another professor's destabilizing conduct as a member of his university's board of governors is elevated to an issue of academic freedom by his union and its national office. A university treats LGBTQ students unequally in the name of religious freedom. Students seek to expel producers of carbon and GMOs from their midst through divestment initiatives.

These are stories of division, not differences, and they undermine university values: a commons in which freedom of expression is the paramount value; a commons that privileges conclusions founded on evidence and reason; a commons that is well governed and one free of discrimination; a commons in which civility is valued and practised; and one that discharges its social responsibilities without presuming to pursue social justice. If we have strayed from these values, we have not yet strayed so far that we cannot recover them. We may need some help along the way, but it is a goal worthy of pursuit by all of us.

Notes

Chapter One: Governance and Academic Freedom at UBC: The Jennifer Berdahl Case

1 Peter MacKinnon, *University Leadership and Public Policy in the Twenty-First Century: A President's Perspective* (Toronto: University of Toronto Press, 2014), chap. 8.
2 Jennifer Berdahl, "Did President Arvind Gupta Lose the Masculinity Contest?" http://jberdahl.blogspot.ca/, 8 August 2015.
3 In Canada, most frequently governors; trustees, regents, or directors are also used. They are boards established by legislation or charter with oversight of universities' business affairs and with the appointment of presidents.
4 "Arvind Gupta Resigns as President of UBC after a Year in Office," CBC News, 7 August 2015.
5 Ken MacQueen, "The Acrimony and Enigma of Arvind Gupta's Exit from UBC," *Maclean's*, 18 August 2015.
6 Ibid.
7 Katie Hyslop, "UBC Faculty and Students Protest Board Handling of Gupta Departure," thetyee.ca/News/, 3 February 2016.
8 Gary Mason, "Seismic Changes Ahead for UBC in Wake of Gupta's Departure," *Globe and Mail*, 12 February 2016.
9 Laura Kane, "Stephen Galloway Suspension Shouldn't Have Been Announced: UBC Faculty Association," CBC News, 20 November 2015.
10 "Author Steven Galloway No Longer Employed at UBC following 'Record of Misconduct,'" CBC News, 22 June 2016.
11 Marsha Lederman, "Steven Galloway's Firing Causes Donor to Rethink Gift to UBC," *Globe and Mail*, 28 September 2016.

12 Marsha Lederman, "Atwood, Ondaatje Call for Probe into Firing of UBC Prof," *Globe and Mail*, 15 November 2016.

13 Marsha Lederman, "Steven Galloway Scandal Creates Divisions in the CanLit World," *Globe and Mail*, 18 November 2016.

14 Ibid.

15 CBC News, "Author Steven Galloway, Who Was Fired by UBC, Apologizes through Lawyer," 23 November 2016.

16 See, for example, Wayne Ross, "Gupta's Mysterious Departure Challenges UBC's Reputation for Open Dialogue," *Vancouver Observer*, 17 August 2015.

17 University Act, RSBC, 1996, c 468, s 60.

18 Collective Agreement between the University of British Columbia and the Faculty Association of the University of British Columbia, Article 10.

19 Kevin Drews, "UBC Faculty Calls for Resignation of John Montalbano," globalnews.ca, 19 August 2015.

20 Privacy Act, RSBC, 1996, c 373.

21 Ibid., s 1(1).

22 Ibid., s 1(2).

23 Lynn Smith, "Summary of the Fact-Finding Process and Conclusions regarding Alleged Breaches of Academic Freedom and Other University Policies at the University of British Columbia," 15 October 2015, 2.

24 Ibid., 3, 4.

25 Universities Canada, Statement on Academic Freedom.

26 Canadian Association of University Teachers, Statement on Academic Freedom.

27 Robert G. Thomas, Collective Agreements of Canadian Universities (2015).

28 Smith, "Summary," n23, 6.

29 The measures include: hire a specialist to work proactively throughout the university to safeguard and preserve academic freedom; create an education program on academic freedom for new faculty and administrators; develop an online tool on academic freedom; and develop a module on academic freedom for all new governors and senators.

30 "UBC Faculty Association Votes 'No Confidence' in Board of Governors," CBC News, 28 January 2016.

31 Katie Hyslop, "UBC Faculty Launch Board of Governors No Confidence Vote," thetyee.ca, 3 March 2016.

32 Joanne Lee-Young, "University of B.C. Appoints Santa Ono as New President," *Vancouver Sun*, 13 June 2016.

33 Stuart Belkin and Martha Piper, "Statement on Board Governance at UBC," April 2016.

Chapter Two: Sexual Transgressions at Dalhousie:
Dentistry Students on Facebook

1 *Report of the Task Force on Misogyny, Sexism and Homophobia in Dalhousie University Faculty of Dentistry*, 2015, 7.
2 Ibid.
3 Halifax Regional Police reviewed the posts and determined that they did not violate the Criminal Code. "Dalhousie Dentistry Scandal Won't Result in Police Charges," CBC News, 15 January 2015.
4 The Royal College of Dental Surgeons of Ontario asked Dalhousie to name the Facebook group members. Its registrar stated that the college is "concerned that if these students, soon to be doctors, if they applied for a licence here in Ontario, we would want to know who they are." "Dalhousie Won't Release Names of Dentistry Facebook Participants," CBC News, 6 January 2015.
5 *Report of the Task Force*, 7.
6 Ibid., 13, 14.
7 Letter from four women in Dentistry's class of 2015 to Dalhousie President Richard Florizone, 6 January 2015, CBC News, 6 January 2016.
8 *Report of the Task Force*, 14.
9 John DeMont, "Dental Students' Fate Tough to Decide," *Chronicle Herald*, 5 January 2015.
10 Senate Discipline Committee Jurisdiction and Procedures, s 17.
11 Literally "in the place of a parent," Dalhousie's Code of Student Conduct stipulates that the university does not stand in loco parentis to its students: "In the exercise of its disciplinary authority, the university treats students as adults, free to organize their own personal lives, behaviour and associations subject only to the law, and to university regulations that are necessary to protect the integrity and proper functioning of the academic and non-academic programs and activities of the University, or its faculties, schools and departments; the peaceful and safe enjoyment of University facilities by other members of the University and the public; the freedom of members of the University to participate reasonably in the programs of the University and in activities on the university's premises; [and] the property of the university or its members."
12 The *Globe and Mail*'s Martin O'Malley was the origin of a statement widely attributed to Pierre Elliott Trudeau when, as minister of justice, he spoke on the decriminalization of homosexuality: "There's no place for the state in the bedrooms of the nation."

13 A sufficient interest in a dispute to allow a complaint to be made and representation to be heard.

14 Freedom of Information and Protection of Privacy Act, 1993, c 5.

15 See nn3 and 4 above.

16 "Research suggests that many victims continue to see sexual victimization as a private matter and most do not disclose their victimization to a formal source ... Given that only a small proportion of sexual offences are formally documented, the prevalence of sexual assault in Canada has been difficult to quantify." Shannon Brennan and Andrea Taylor-Butts, *Sexual Assault in Canada 2004–2007* (Ottawa: Canadian Centre for Justice Statistics, 2008), 7.

17 Rachel Browne, "Why Don't Canadian Universities Want to Talk about Sexual Assault?" *MacLean's*, 30 October 2014; Laura Kane, "Canadian University Students Say Universities Dragging Heels on Sex Assault Policies," Huffpost British Columbia, 7 August 2016.

18 McGill Draft Policy against Sexual Violence, 2016.

19 Ian Bailey, "UBC to Consider Banning Relationships between Faculty and Students," *Globe and Mail*, 20 April 2016.

20 Academica Group, "UBC Faculty, CAUT Show Differing Levels of Openness toward Bans on Student–Teacher Relationships," 28 April 2016.

21 "Yale Bans Sex between Students and Faculty," *New York Times*, 15 November 1997.

22 "Harvard Bans Sex between Professors and Undergraduates," USA Today Network, 5 February 2015.

23 "Consensual Romantic or Sexual Relationships between Faculty, Staff and Students," Northwestern University, 2014. Section 2 of the policy notes that consensual romantic relations "between faculty and students or coaches and students, even absent any supervisory or evaluative authority, may lead to unanticipated conflicts of interest since a teacher's or coach's influence and power may extend beyond the classroom." When undergraduates are involved, "the difference between institutional power and the inherent risk of coercion are so great that no faculty member or coaching staff member shall enter into a romantic, dating or sexual relationship with a Northwestern undergraduate student, regardless of whether there is a supervisory or evaluative relationship between them."

24 Don Clairmont and Anthony Thomson, "The Nova Scotia Restorative Justice Initiative: A System-Level Approach," 2001.

25 *Report of the Task Force*, 80.

26 *Report from the Restorative Justice Process at the Dalhousie University Faculty of Dentistry*, 2015, 27.

27 Ibid.
28 Ibid., 31.
29 Ibid.
30 Ibid., 13, 14.
31 Ibid., 14.
32 Ibid., 15.
33 Ibid.
34 Ibid., 8.
35 Ibid.
36 Ibid., 10.
37 In 2013 Jim Turk, executive director of the Canadian Association of University Teachers, acknowledged that it is rare for a tenured professor to be fired at a Canadian university. See Graeme Hamilton, "Tenured McGill University Professor Fired after Accounting 'Twirps' Uncover $159,500 in Improper Spending," *National Post*, 19 March 2013. But it is not rare for Canadian university presidents to be dismissed. Reliable estimates indicate that since 2003 about one-quarter of Canada's ninety-six universities have seen presidents discharged from their offices. See Leo Charbonneau, "The (Continued) Revolving Door at the Top of Canada's Universities," *University Affairs*, 28 November 2012.
38 "An Alternative Approach to Campus Justice," editorial, *New York Times*, 9 September 2015; "Dalhousie's Handling of Facebook Scandal Is the Right Way to Go," editorial, *Globe and Mail*, 5 January 2015.
39 Editorial, *Globe and Mail*, 5 January 2015.

Chapter Three: Safe Space, Comfort, and Freedom of Expression: Stories from across Canada

1 [2001] 1 SCR 45, at para 23 (SCC).
2 Kent Roach and David Schneiderman, "Freedom of Expression in Canada" (2013), 61 SCLR (2d), 429.
3 Steven Chase, "Ann Coulter's Speech in Ottawa Cancelled," *Globe and Mail*, 23 March 2010.
4 Ingrid Peritz, "Israel's Netanyahu Greeted with Violence in Montreal," *Globe and Mail*, 10 September 2002.
5 "University of Ottawa Rejects Ann Coulter," *Ubyssey*, 25 March 2010.
6 Bruce Cheadle, "Ann Coulter Gets Cold Shoulder in Ottawa," *Globe and Mail*, 22 March 2010.
7 "University of Ottawa Rejects Ann Coulter."

8 Reproduced in Christopher Brennan, "University of Chicago Dean Sends Students Letter against 'Trigger Warnings' and 'Safe Spaces,'" *New York Daily News*, 26 August 2016.

9 University of Calgary Student Non-Academic Misconduct Policy, s 4.10(e), qtd in *Wilson v University of Calgary*, (2014) ABQB 190, 3.

10 *Wilson v University of Calgary*, (2014) ABQB 190.

11 Canadian Charter of Rights and Freedoms, s 32(1).

12 *McKinney v University of Guelph* [1990] 3 SCR 229.

13 *Eldridge v British Columbia (AG)* [1997] 3 SCR 624.

14 *Pridgen v University of Calgary*, (2012) ABCA 139, per Strekaf J.

15 *Wilson v University of Calgary*, n10 at 35.

16 Ibid., 31.

17 Ibid., 2.

18 Also the title of Ronald Dworkin's seminal volume *Taking Rights Seriously* (Cambridge, MA: Harvard University Press, 1978).

19 *Cool Runnings*, Walt Disney Pictures, 1993.

20 Jill Mahoney, "Students Cause Uproar with Blackface for Halloween," *Globe and Mail*, 11 November 2009.

21 Denise Balkisson, "How a Halloween Getup Went Badly Wrong," *Toronto Star*, 12 November 2009.

22 Mahoney, "Students Cause Uproar."

23 Ibid.

24 "Brock University Students in Blackface Win Halloween Contest," CBC News, 4 November 2014.

25 Morgan Dotson, "Students Protest Admin Response to Campus Party," *Queen's Journal*, 1 December 2016.

26 Ibid.

27 Tu Thanh Ha, "Paul Bronfman 'Outraged' over Pro-Palestinian Mural at York University," *Globe and Mail*, 26 January, 2016.

28 Ibid.

29 Although there were reports of rioters being charged with disciplinary offences at Concordia, the writer could not locate any record of findings or penalties for the students at either Concordia or Ottawa.

30 Quoted in Jonathan Gatehouse, "How a Cancelled Yoga Class Stretches the Point on Cultural Appropriation," *Maclean's*, 23 November 2015.

31 Marina von Stackelberg, "Laurentian University Professor Removed for Asking Students to Agree to Profane Language," CBC News, 4 January 2016.

32 Ibid.

33 Douglas Quan, "Laurentian University Professor Loses Class after Asking Students to Sign Form Allowing Offensive Language," *National Post*, 5 January 2016.
34 Peter Edwards, "Laurentian University Prof Yanked over Waiver to Students Warning of Crude Language in Class," *Toronto Star*, 5 January 2016.
35 Ibid.
36 Tom Yun, "U of T Community Responds to Jordan Peterson on Gender Identities," *Varsity*, 3 October 2016.
37 Sean Craig, "U of T Professor Attacks Political Correctness, Says He Refuses to Use Genderless Pronouns," *National Post*, 28 September 2016.
38 Simona Chiose, "Jordan Peterson and the Trolls in the Ivory Tower," *Globe and Mail*, 20 October 2016.
39 Ibid.
40 Christie Blatchford, "Incident behind Ryerson Anti-Racism Protests Hardly Black and White," *National Post*, 28 November 2016.
41 Amira Zubairi, "School of Social Work Director Steps Down," *Ryersonian*, 29 November 2016.
42 Geoff Smith, "Trigger Warnings: The Latest Threat to Academic Freedom," *Globe and Mail*, 4 April 2014.
43 Andrew Potter, "How a Snowstorm Exposed Quebec's Real Problem: Social Malaise," *Maclean's*, 20 March 2017.
44 Jonathan Montpetit, "Quebec Premier Lashes Out at *Maclean's* for Suggesting Province Is in State of 'Serious Dysfunction,'" CBC News, 21 March 2017.
45 Potter resignation statement, 22 March 2017.
46 "Message from the Principal and Vice-Chancellor of McGill University," 23 March 2017.
47 See chapters 1 and 4.
48 At Wilfrid Laurier University, Sandor Dosman had rented space from the Graduate Students Association for his Veritas Cafe for nearly five years. His tongue-in-cheek Help Wanted ad indicated he was looking for a "slave" to help run his shop and that the pay is "crap." His contract was immediately terminated by the student association. The university announced support for the decision, saying it was all about making the university an "inclusive, welcoming and respectful place." "GSA Releases Third Statement," *Cord*, 14 December 2016.
    At the University of British Columbia, President Santa Ono apologized to John Furlong, former CEO of the 2010 Vancouver Olympics, after a

speech he was scheduled to give at the university was cancelled. The cancellation appears to have come in the wake of unsubstantiated allegations of sexual assault against Mr Furlong. He was subsequently reinstated as the speaker for the 28 February 2017 event. Glen Korstrom, "UBC Reinstates John Furlong as Keynote Speaker," *Business Vancouver*, 9 January 2017.

At St Francis Xavier University a student objected to the selection of Jian Ghomeshi's defence lawyer, Marie Henein, as a guest speaker, saying that she would "silence victims and perpetuate rape culture." She complained about Henein's cross-examinations of the complainants and asked that the speech be cancelled. "We instituted a new sexual violence policy and then to have it go hand-in-hand with this lecture is kind of like saying one thing and doing another." "Ghomeshi's Lawyer Marie Henein to Speak to Universities Despite Opposition Her Talk Exacerbates 'Rape Culture,'" *National Post*, 10 February 2017.

49 "Yes, I'd lie to you," *Economist*, 10–16 September 2016.

Chapter Four: Academic Freedom and Governance – A Reprise: Carleton's Blogging Board Member

1 CAUT news release, 14 December 2015.
2 Council of Graduate Students Association, Carleton University, 8 December 2015.
3 Chris Cobb, "Prof Refuses to Sign Agreement, Carleton Faces Censure over Secrecy Order," *Ottawa Citizen*, 14 December 2015.
4 Saskatchewan might appear to be an exception with five of eleven board members at the Universities of Regina and Saskatchewan appointed by the provincial government. However, both universities have tricameral governance systems, with their senates being external bodies. The two Senate members and five government appointees at these universities give them each seven of eleven external members.
5 Often attributed to Edmund Burke, the distinction holds that the delegates must do the bidding of those who commissioned them to act on their behalf, whereas representatives are free to act on their judgment and consciences.
6 Gorelick Blog, Carletonbogblog.wordpress.com, 10 October 2013.
7 Ibid., 13 April 2015.
8 Ibid., 8 May 2015.
9 Ibid., 22 June 2015.
10 Ibid., 26 June 2015.

11 Ibid., 29 June 2015.
12 Ibid., 13 November 2015.
13 Ibid., 28 December 2015.
14 Ibid., 26 January 2016.
15 Ibid., 12 February 2016.
16 Ibid., 21 March 2016.
17 Ibid., 26 May 2016.
18 Statement on Academic Freedom, Universities Canada, 2011.
19 Ibid.
20 CAUT Statement on Academic Freedom, 2011.
21 Ralph E. Fuchs, "Academic Freedom: Its Basic Philosophy, Function and History," *Law and Contemporary Problems* 28 (1963): 435.
22 Ibid., 436.
23 Ibid.
24 American Association of University Professors' 1940 Statement of Principles of Academic Freedom and Tenure.
25 Joint conferences between the American Association of University Professors and the Association of American Colleges (now the Association of American Colleges and Universities) began in 1934, and both parties agreed upon the 1940 statement.
26 Constitution of the United States First Amendment (1791): "Congress shall make no law respecting an establishment of religion, or prohibiting the free exercise thereof; or abridging the freedom of speech, or of the press; or the right of the people peaceably to assemble, and to petition the government for a redress of grievances."
27 The Collective Agreement between Carleton University and the Carleton University Academic Staff Association 2014–2017, Article 4.
28 Lynn Smith, "Summary of the Fact-Finding Process and Conclusions regarding Alleged Breaches of Academic Freedom and Other University Policies at the University of British Columbia," 2015.
29 Ibid., 6. The University of Saskatchewan's guidelines for board member responsibilities include the following: "By accepting a position on the Board of Governors, faculty members acknowledge that they will participate under constraints which do not apply to faculty at large (for example, constraints around confidentiality). Moreover, their 'freedom to criticize the University' takes a different form while they serve as a member of the board. On the one hand, that freedom is strengthened because of the direct access that the individual has to the board, access that is much greater than most members of the academic community enjoy. On the other hand, the freedom is limited by the duty of loyalty, which

stipulates that a decision taken by the board is a group decision and must be publicly supported by all board members."

30 Gorelick continued to post to his blog after his board term concluded. He attends public board meetings as an observer.

Chapter Five: Freedom of Religion in the Commons: A Law School for Trinity Western University?

1 "The Mission of Trinity Western University," Trinity Western University, www.twu.ca/about.

2 *Trinity Western University v The Law Society of British Columbia*, 2016 BCCA 423.

3 *BC Gov News*, 18 December 2013.

4 The Canadian Council of Law Deans was an early opponent of the initiative. In 2013 the council wrote to the Federation of Law Societies, "The Covenant specifically contemplates that gay, lesbian or bisexual students may be subject to disciplinary measures including expulsion. This is a matter of great concern for all the members of the CCLD. Discrimination on the basis of sexual orientation is unlawful in Canada and fundamentally at odds with the core values of all Canadian law schools." "Submissions to the Federation regarding the Proposed Accreditation of Trinity Western University's Law Program," flsc.ca/resouces/canadian-common-law-approval-status. See also revision, p. 108.

Growing opposition to the proposed new school did not go unanswered. Trinity Western University President Bob Kuhn said that the opposition to the new law school signalled a new era of persecution against Christians and their views. "New Persecution Coming, Trinity Western President Warns," www christianweek.com, 27 March 2014.

5 James Bradshaw, "Lawyers Challenge B.C. Approval of Trinity Western Law School," *Globe and Mail*, 14 April 2014.

6 "Trinity Western Law School: B.C. Law Society Members Vote to Reverse Approval," CBC News, 30 October 2014.

7 *BC GovNews*, 11 December 2014.

8 Global News, 18 December, 2014.

9 *Trinity Western University v The Law Society of British Columbia*, 2015 BCSC 2326.

10 Ibid.

11 Ibid., n2.

12 Ibid., 7.

13 Ibid., 12.

14 Ibid., 65.
15 2015 NSSC 25.
16 2016 NSCA 59.
17 *Trinity Western University v The Law Society of Upper Canada*, 2016 ONCA 518, para 69.
18 Ibid., para 71.
19 Ibid., para 79.
20 Ibid., para 101.
21 Ibid., para 109.
22 Ibid.
23 Ibid., para 141.
24 *Trinity Western University v British Columbia College of Teachers* [2001] SCR 772.
25 Ibid., para 36.
26 Ibid., n14.
27 For example, Acadia and Brandon Universities (Baptist), several Catholic universities and colleges, Mount Allison University (United Church).
28 William Bruneau, "Academic Freedom and Religious Conviction at Canada's Faith-Based Universities and Colleges," in *Academic Freedom in Conflict: The Struggle over Free Speech Rights in the University*, ed. J.L. Turk, 145–71 (Toronto: Lorimer, 2014).
29 Ibid., 149.
30 Amendment to By-Law Number One Being the General By-Law Regulating the Transaction of the Business and Affairs of Universities Canada (2016).
31 I must disclose my involvement in this process. I served as chair of the Association of Universities and Colleges of Canada from 2003 to 2005, and subsequently as chair of its standing committee that dealt with constitutional and regulatory matters. While I was not involved in drafting the 2016 amendment, I was a participant in many of the discussions on this topic, particularly in 2011 and 2012. I can personally attest to the frequent and lengthy discussions on this subject, both in committee and plenary sessions.
32 Note 30.
33 Justice Peter Cory's summary of the facts in *Vriend v Alberta* [1998] 1 SCR 493 at para 7.
34 Ibid.
35 Following the admission of King's to membership in 1992, AUCC assigned to its standing committee on constitutional affairs (SACAB) the task of reviewing the membership requirements as they might apply

to faith-based institutions. In 1994 the committee recommended, and the membership approved, this criterion: "Where an institution meets all other requirements for the admission to the AUCC but requires adherence to a statement of faith and/or a code of conduct that might constitute a constraint upon academic freedom ... such an institution may nevertheless be admitted to the Association provided that the conditions of membership in that university community ... are made clear to staff and students prior to employment or admission as the case may be."

The issue remain quiescent until 2003, when it was again considered after a moratorium was placed on membership of faith-based institutions. The moratorium was soon lifted, and the association received applications for membership from Tyndale University College and Crandall (formerly Atlantic Baptist) University. Following rejection of the former, AUCC's Board established an ad hoc committee on membership issues, which resulted in 2008 in six recommendations, two of which are germane here: "AUCC should draw a distinction between belief and practice, emphasizing that the freedom to hold beliefs is broader than the freedom to act upon them," and "Faith-based institutions and other prospective members that adhere to and act in conformity with the AUCC Statement on Academic Freedom and Institutional Autonomy may be members of AUCC."

Subsequently, AUCC's member institutions turned down an AUCC Board recommendation – on a close vote – to admit Crandall University to membership. They did so on the basis of a potential for that institution to discriminate against LGBTQ persons, and so debate on membership continued, though now the ground had shifted from academic freedom to possible discrimination at what were now five faith-based members of the organization. There would be further rounds of debate, legal advice, and more debate before AUCC's successor organization, Universities Canada, arrived at the 2016 criterion and policy.

36 See, for example, "Powerful, Faceless Bureaucrats Attack Religious Freedom of Faith-Based Universities in Canada," *Culture Witness*, 25 September 2016; "Major Canadian Universities Push Anti-Christian Hiring Policies on Small Faith-Based Schools," *Life Site*, 22 September 2016; "Universities Canada's Proposed Anti-Discrimination Policy May Hurt Faith-Based Schools," *BC Catholic*, 21 September 2016.

37 Universities Canada Policy Statement, 2016.

38 Ibid.

39 Ibid.

40 Faith statements and requirements related to them raise issues of both discrimination and of academic freedom. While the former is the focus of the Trinity Western law school case and the discussion here, the latter remains relevant to freedom from discrimination argument. Trinity Western's policy on academic freedom states that the university "is committed to academic freedom in teaching and investigation from a stated perspective, i.e., within parameters consistent with the confessional basis of the constituency to which the university is responsible." This is a departure from academic freedom as I have considered the subject in this volume and in my previous book, *University Leadership and Public Policy in the Twenty-First Century*. It raises the question whether academic freedom is ever compatible with faith statements. See Bruneau, "Academic Freedom and Religious Conviction."

41 Peter B. Wood, "It's Time to Talk about Defunding Universities That Won't Defend Freedom of Speech," *Federalist*, 8 February 2017.

42 Motion 103 calls on the Government of Canada to "condemn Islamophobia and all forms of systematic racism and religious discrimination," asks the government to "recognize the need to quell the increasing public climate of hate and fear," and requests that the Commons Heritage Committee "study how the government could develop a government-wide approach to reducing or eliminating systemic racism and religious discrimination, including Islamophobia, and collect data to provide context for hate crime reports and to conduct needs assessments for impacted communities."

Chapter Six: Making the World a Better Place:
The Social Responsibility of Canadian Universities

1 Clark Kerr, *The Uses of the University*, 5th ed. (Cambridge, MA: Harvard University Press, 2001).

2 George Fallis, *Multiversities, Ideas and Democracy* (Toronto: University of Toronto Press, 2007), 343.

3 Ibid., 344.

4 Ibid., 350.

5 Ibid., 351.

6 Ibid., 352.

7 Ibid., 347.

8 Ibid., 341.

9 Calls for the academic boycott of Israel are a prominent contemporary example.

10 George Leef, "Should University Presidents Speak Out?" See Thru Edu, 19 March 2013, http://www.seethruedu.com/updatesshould-university-presidents-speak-out/.

11 Karen Gross, "Speak Out," *Inside Higher Ed*, 2 March 2015.

12 I should disclose my engagement with the challenges here. When I became president of the University of Saskatchewan in 1999, one of the installation speakers was Perry Bellegarde, then chief of the Federation of Saskatchewan Indian Nations and, since 2014, national chief of the Assembly of First Nations. In his remarks Chief Bellegarde used the metaphor of "the new buffalo" and the idea it represents became a priority for my thirteen years in office.

Soon after taking office, the president of the Saskatchewan Indian Federated College (subsequently renamed First Nations University of Canada) suggested that his college assume responsibility for educating the University of Saskatchewan's Indigenous students. I declined the invitation in favour of emphasizing Aboriginal access across the broad range of the university's thirteen colleges, and turned to George Lafond, the former chief of the Saskatoon Tribal Council, to join my office as Aboriginal advisor, the first such university office in Canada. He led our initiatives with considerable success. More than 10 per cent of the university's 20,000 plus students are Indigenous, and they are enrolled in all colleges. The university's past chancellor is Aboriginal, and there have been two successive Indigenous student union leaders. The new Gordon Oakes Red Bear Student Centre, designed by Douglas Cardinal, has taken its place in the midst of the university's traditional collegiate gothic architecture.

13 Ibid. See also Blair Stonechild, *The New Buffalo: The Struggle for Aboriginal Post-Secondary Education in Canada* (Winnipeg: University of Manitoba Press, 2006).

14 Truth and Reconciliation Commission of Canada, *Final Report*, Ottawa, 2015.

15 Statement of Apology to former students of Indian Residential Schools, Ottawa, 11 June 2008.

16 I first encountered the word *newcomer* in this context in the work of historian J.R. Miller. See, for example, J.R. Miller, *Reflections on Native-Newcomer Relations: Selected Essays* (Toronto: University of Toronto Press, 2004).

17 Statement of Apology, n8.

18 Calls to Action 43 and 44 are as follows:

43. We call upon federal, provincial, municipal and territorial governments to fully adopt and implement the United Nations Declaration on the Rights of Indigenous Peoples as the framework for reconciliation.

44. We call upon the government of Canada to develop a national action plan, strategies and other concrete measures to achieve the goals of the United Nations Declaration on the Rights of Indigenous Peoples.

Nevertheless, in 2010 the Canadian Government endorsed the declaration with the proviso that it is "a non-legally binding document that does not reflect customary international law, nor change Canadian laws" ("Canada Endorses Indigenous Rights Declaration," CBC News, 12 November 2010). Clearly the endorsement falls short of TRC Calls to Action 43 and 44.

19 Article 3 of the UN Declaration states, "Indigenous peoples have the right to self-determination. By virtue of that right they freely determine their political status." Beginning with this article, and with several others, the declaration has far-reaching and still unresolved implications for the Canadian state and relationships among its peoples. Clarity about the status of the declaration is necessary before a decision "to fully adopt and implement" as called for by the TRC.

20 Prime Minister Trudeau promised to "fully implement the Calls to Action of the Truth and Reconciliation Commission, starting with the implementation of the United Nations Declaration on the Rights of Indigenous Peoples." Statement of the Office of the Prime Minister of Canada, 15 December 2015.

21 Wecheehetowin (Working Together in Cree), *Final Report of the Steering Committee for the University of Toronto Response to the Truth and Reconciliation Commission of Canada* (Toronto, 2017).

22 Ibid., 7.

23 *TRC Report*, note 7, Call to Action 24.

24 Ibid., Call to Action 28.

25 The Bora Laskin Faculty of Law at Lakehead University is Canada's newest law school, and its first new one in forty-four years. With its Northern Ontario regional focus and unique mission, it has worked closely with the Anishnabek Nation, the Métis Nation of Ontario, and the Nishnawbe Nation. One of its compulsory classes is Law 2000: Aboriginal Legal Issues, though the school's mission in Aboriginal and Indigenous Law

is reflected across the full three-year curriculum, in its impressive building in Thunder Bay, and in the commitment of its dean, Angelique Eagle-Woman.

26 "Carolyn Bennett Joins Call for Mandatory Aboriginal Studies Course," *Varsity*, 1 February 2016.

27 *TRC Report*, note 14, Call to Action 16.

28 The approach here is aligned with 14(iv) of the *TRC Report*: "The preservation, revitalization and strengthening of Aboriginal languages and cultures are best managed by Aboriginal people and communities."

29 Ibid.

30 World Health Organization, "Indigenous Peoples and Participatory Health Research" (draft), 2003.

31 "Tri-Council Policy Statement: Ethical Conduct for Research Involving Humans," 2014.

32 There remain questions about Indigenous–non-Indigenous relationships going forward. We have seen that there is uncertainty about the interpretation and legal status of the UN Declaration on the Rights of Indigenous Peoples. Fundamentally the question is about the degree of its emphasis on separateness, as distinct from common citizenship. An emphasis on the latter may be more likely to generate the political will and financial commitments required for the tasks ahead.

33 Amanda Leslie, "Dal Students Show Support for Fossil Fuel Divestment," *unews*, 11 February 2014.

34 Dalhousie University Board of Governors, "Fossil Fuel Divestment Statement," November 2014.

35 Ibid.

36 DivestDal Facebook post, divestdal.ca, 7 April 2015.

37 Mychaylo Prystupa, "Fossil Fuel Investment Fever Hits Canadian Campuses," *National Observer*, 25 January 2015.

38 "University of British Columbia Endowment Responsible Investment Policy Committee Terms of Reference," treasury.ubc.ca.

39 Food Democracy Now!, www.fooddemocracynow.org.

40 Kristen Schmitt, "Five Ways to Divest from Monsanto," UTNE, 17 July 2013.

Chapter Seven: Conclusion

1 James Duff and Robert Berdahl, *University Government in Canada: Report of a Commission Sponsored by the Canadian Association of University Teachers*

and the Association of Universities and Colleges of Canada (Toronto: University of Toronto Press, 1966).

2 Glen A. Jones, Theresa Shanahan, and Paul Goyan, "University Governance in Canadian Higher Education," *Tertiary Education and Management* 7, no. 2 (2001): 135–48.

3 Ibid., 2.

4 Bicameralism is the prevailing model, though not the universal one. In 1972 the University of Toronto adopted a unicameral model in the form of its new governing council, though bicameral influence may continue in its committee structure. Some universities (Saskatchewan, Regina) have a tricameral system with boards, academically councils and senates that are primarily external bodies.

5 Jones, Shanahan, and Goyan, "University Governance," note 3.

6 Ibid.

7 Ibid., 2, 3.

8 I previously reported that a review of international rankings reveals that top-ranked institutions do not have faculty unions. Nor do the Canadian universities that feature most prominently in them. McGill, McMaster, and the Universities of Toronto and Waterloo do not have faculty unions. The Universities of Alberta and British Columbia are subject to statutory regimes that mean that their faculty associations are non-unionized. Of course non-unionized faculty associations may sometimes see themselves as unions and conduct themselves accordingly. I witnessed this at Athabasca University, where the non-unionized faculty association adopted a stance of relentless adversarialism in its relationship with the administration and board of governors. MacKinnon, *University Leadership and Public Policy in the Twenty-First Century*, 99.

9 Ibid., 100, 101.

10 We should greet motions of non-confidence that are unanimously passed in large groups in different meetings with the same scepticism that we bring to election results in one-party political regimes. At Carleton, it was reported that several unions and associations passed unanimous motions of non-confidence in the university's board of governors. When everyone is thinking and voting the same way, it is usually because tolerance for differences is absent.

11 "Dalhousie Must Act Decisively in Dentistry Misogyny," *Chronicle Herald* (Halifax), 22 December 2014.

12 Kim Campbell, "How Journalism Will Protect Our Democracy in the Era of Fake News," *Globe and Mail*, 15 February 2017.

13 Chapter 3, n48 of this volume.

14 Chapter 3, n2 of this volume.

15 Chapter 5, n4 of this volume.

16 I am indebted to Professor Tamara Buckwold of the University of Alberta, who raised this argument with me in our correspondence on the TWU case.

17 Ross Paul, *Leadership under Fire: The Challenging Role of a Canadian University President* (Montreal and Kingston: McGill-Queen's University Press, 2011); Stephen Trachtenberg, Gerald B. Kauver, and E. Grady Bogue, *Presidencies Derailed: Why University Leaders Fail and How to Prevent It* (Baltimore: Johns Hopkins University Press, 2013); MacKinnon, *University Leadership and Public Policy in the Twenty-First Century.*

18 Names that come quickly to mind are the Rt. Hon. David Johnson (McGill, Waterloo); Paul Davenport (University of Alberta, Western); Robert Lacroix (University of Montreal); Heather Munroe-Blum (McGill); Martha Piper (UBC); Rob Pritchard (University of Toronto); Indira Samarasekera (University of Alberta); and Tom Traves (Dalhousie, Brock).

19 L. Pennock, G.A. Jones, J.M. Leclerc, and Sharon X. Li, "Assessing the Role and Structure of Academic Senates in Canadian Universities, 2000–2012," *Canadian Journal of Higher Education* 70 (2015): 503–18; L. Pennock, G.A. Jones, J.M. Leclerc, and Sharon X. Li, "Challenges and Opportunities for Collegial Governance at Canadian Universities: Reflections on a Survey of Academic Senates," *Canadian Journal of Higher Education* 46, no. 3 (2016): 73–89.

20 Pennock et al., "Assessing the Role and Structure of Academic Senates."

21 Ibid.

22 Ibid.

23 Pennock et al., "Challenges and Opportunities for Collegial Governance," 73.

24 Ibid., 86.

25 Ibid.

26 This subject is more fully explored in MacKinnon, *University Leadership and Public Policy in the Twenty-First Century*, chap. 1, n1.

27 *Report of the CAUT Ad Hoc Advisory Committee on Governance*, 2009, 3.

28 "CAUT Policy Statement on Governance," 2008.

29 "Governance on the Rocks," *CAUT Bulletin*, March 2017. The statement was attributed to executive director David Robinson.

30 Ibid.

Index